Pleasures Forevermore

Phillip Keller

HARVEST HOUSE PUBLISHERS
Eugene, Oregon 97402

Scripture quotations are from the King James Version of the Bible.

PLEASURES FOREVERMORE

Copyright © 1992 by Harvest House Publishers
Eugene, Oregon 97402

Library of Congress Cataloging-in-Publication Data

Keller, W. Phillip (Weldon Phillip), 1920–
    Pleasures forevermore / Phillip Keller.
    ISBN 1-56507-025-9
    1. Meditations.   2. Keller, W. Phillip (Weldon Phillip), 1920–   .   I. Title.
    BV4832.2.K4155   1992
    242—dc20   92-5552
                                                                                    CIP

To
Richard and Fern,
dear, dear friends
who have helped so much
to make this book possible.

Acknowledgments

In large part this work has been possible because of the generous kindness shown to me by two precious people during the past year.

Richard Webber, entirely on his own, came and offered to turn our bare-boned basement into a serene sanctuary and splendid office where I could work so energetically.

Fern Webber, in the same generous spirit, offered to type the manuscripts for both *God Is My Delight* and *Pleasures Forevermore*. This she has done with expertise and loving care. I am so deeply grateful for their part in the project.

Again, I wish to thank those special people who pray for me so faithfully—some every day, some very far away. How their love and interest has sustained me across the years!

Because this book is about the simple life that Ursula and I share, I here express my warm love and gentle thanks to her. She and I have been through many an adventure with God our Father.

Most of all I am grateful to Christ Himself for enriching my life in such wondrous ways of His own delightful design. This book is about just that!

—W. Phillip Keller

Books by W. Phillip Keller

Splendor from the Sea

As a Tree Grows

Bold Under God—a Fond Look at a Frontier Preacher

A Shepherd Looks at Psalm 23

A Layman Looks at the Lord's Prayer

Rabboni—Which Is to Say, Master

A Shepherd Looks at the Good Shepherd and His Sheep

A Gardener Looks at the Fruits of the Spirit

Mighty Man of Valor—Gideon

Mountain Splendor

Taming Tension

Expendable

Still Waters

A Child Looks at Psalm 23

Ocean Glory

Walking with God

On Wilderness Trails

Elijah—Prophet of Power

Salt for Society

A Layman Looks at the Lamb of God

Lessons from a Sheep Dog

Wonder o' the Wind

Joshua—Mighty Warrior and Man of Faith

A Layman Looks at the Love of God

Sea Edge

David I

David II

Sky Edge

Chosen Vessels

In the Master's Hands

The High Cost of Holiness
  (**formerly** *Predators in Our Pulpits*

Songs of My Soul

Thank You, Father

God Is My Delight

Pleasures Forevermore

CONTENTS

How It All Began

It was late on New Year's Eve 1990. Heavy snow had been falling all day. Roads were blocked and travel was hazardous. So Cheri (my wife's pet name) and I decided to spend the evening quietly in the warm comfort of our home.

As the hours passed I felt an inner tug at my spirit to take out a writing pad and jot down a list of the gracious, pleasant events that had occurred during the year. Somehow I felt there would only be a handful of heartening episodes, since 1990 had been a very tough and trying year. Both of us had been very ill; it was a year when one difficulty after another had arisen to test our strength. There had been frustrations galore, and many fine plans had been set aside.

However, I began to make my list, to jog my memory, to relive the moments when hope and cheer and faith in my Father sprang into life renewed. As I wrote down the events it startled me to find my memory spurred on and on, until more than 30 beautiful bonuses covered both sides of my sheet of paper. Surely we had been the recipients of rich benefits all year. And though so late, an upwelling stream of gratitude flowed from my soul. This was the "silver edge" to life.

At dawn on New Year's morning I asked my Father to impress upon me what special service I could offer Him and others in the year ahead. "Son, search for the silver linings in life!" The thought came clear and concisely. "Recount in writing the lovely things I do for you through-out this year. They will be a double blessing: first for you in your advanced age (past 70 now), and secondly for all others who read of my kindness to you."

So it is that I began to do my Father's bidding.

New Year's Eve Beneath a Blue Moon

*T*HE EVENING OF WHICH I WROTE at the beginning of this book was approaching midnight. Suddenly the doorbell rang out its welcome sound. I opened it to be met by the warm muzzle of a beautiful big Golden Labrador. He greeted me fondly, rubbing his handsome head against my thigh and shaking the snow from his back with swift contortions of his tail.

Just beyond him stood his owners, neighbors who lived just up the road. They were bundled up in heavy boots and warm overcoats. "We're off for a tramp through the snow. The clouds are parting. Look at the beautiful blue moon!" I looked up to see the full moon, veiled in fine mist, swinging out from behind a cloud bank.

It was in truth the night of a blue moon, and only rarely are there ever two full moons in the same month. But on this New Year's Eve of 1990 that unusual event took place. Nor would it happen again for 19 years, in late 2009.

Our friends chatted with us a few moments. Then we agreed to meet at their house just before midnight to share the happy occasion. They were off into the night, the great dog bounding around them with pure ecstasy.

Quickly Cheri made up an attractive plate of home-made cookies, Christmas cake, and chocolates. We pulled on warm socks and sweaters, laced on boots, and headed out into the driving wind and snow. Arm-in-arm we braced each other, for there was slick ice beneath the drifts.

In our friends' house a cheerful blaze burned in the fireplace. The big Lab relaxed in his favorite corner, and the fragrance of fresh-brewed tea filled the room.

Quickly our conversation turned into happy, joyous chatter that passes so easily between people fond of each other. Only 18 months before we had been total strangers, when we had moved into this new neighborhood. But since then we had become dear friends who waved and stopped to chat whenever we passed each other's place.

Exactly at midnight we hailed the advent of the new year. With smiles and hugs we gently embraced each other in fond affection. This was the essence of the spirit of goodwill and good cheer. It was the aspect of life that could enable us to face a forbidding future of possible war in the Persian Gulf and a discouraging economic depression throughout the world.

In those memorable moments we were back to basics—a crackling fire, hot cups of tea, joyous laughter, a lovely dog in the corner, footprints in the fresh snow, the warmth of friendship.

> None of it was planned.
> All of it came softly, spontaneously.
> Yet it would remain as a lovely legacy.

Cheri and I stayed only a short time. Then we slipped into our wool coats, bade our friends a fond farewell, and stepped out into the swirling snow.

The blue moon turned the whole countryside into a snow-white winter wonderland. We tramped home in deep contentment. Serenity settled down deep into our souls. This night was one we would long cherish as a precious, jewel-like memory.

Some of our Father's finest gifts come to us wrapped in the unforgettable tissue of gentle surprises and gracious goodwill.

Deep Snow
and
Home-Baked
Bread

$\mathcal{T}$HIS HAS BEEN ONE OF THOSE old-fashioned, biting-cold winters that sear the skin and chill the bones. One has not heard a single comment in months about "the hothouse effect" or "the dangerous warming of the planet." If indeed it is happening, then we wish some of those warm winds and moderate temperatures would move this way! We could use some solar heat with genuine gratitude in our icebound world.

But for me there has been one enormous and lovely benefit that winter weather brings. It is home-baked bread. When the ferocious Arctic Front moves down out of the far north, when the ice winds scream across the lake, when heavy snow blankets this mountain world, Ursula sets to work baking bread.

She is sturdy stock, from the old school, which contends that the first line of defense against weather that can kill a man is ample food on the table. No place here for special diets or meager meals. She prepares steaming bowls of home-made soup, heaped-up plates of succulent roast beef, and beautiful brown loaves of home-baked bread.

The golden loaves come out of the hot oven redolent with that fragrant aroma which only fresh-made bread procures. The whole house is filled with it. As I step in through the door, my cheeks crimson with cold, my clothes sheathed in snow and ice, the whole world is suddenly a wonderful place to be. For there are fresh loaves of golden grain on the kitchen counter.

In profound pleasure and loving gratitude I gather Ursula into my arms, hug her hard, and kiss her cheek. She is the maker of this banquet.

Before the steaming loaves have even cooled, I draw the gleaming bread knife from its drawer. The fresh, crisp crust is sliced open and the exquisite fragrance of the whole wheat grain fills the room. Butter melts in moments, and with a steaming cup of tea in hand I settle back in sheer delight. There is no finer fare in the far north.

Let the north wind howl in the frozen pines outside our windows. Let the frost paint its magic crystal pictures on the glass. Let snow deepen until we are virtually housebound. All is well and all is warm: There is fresh-baked bread—enough to dispel the darkest hues of the winter blues!

Nor is this just the matter of a man satisfying the enormous appetite generated by wind and ice and snow. There is something beyond a purely physical need being met here. Home-baked bread, so seldom found anywhere these days, conveys contentment to us, speaks of security within the walls of our homes, quiets our inner conflicts. It is the bread of life—a life that many of us know little about.

There is a therapy, a healing, a wholeness to home-baked bread. It has been found that some mental patients in psychiatric institutions will respond in wonderful ways if given a chance to work in the bakery and help make home-baked bread.

Are we surprised, then, that our Lord, in His magnificent, brief prayer, requested calmly, "Give us this day our daily bread"? And by that He meant, no doubt, bread freshly made and freshly relished. For, you see, the baking and the breaking of home-made bread is indeed a sacrament. It is the transmission of life itself from God to man by way of soil, sun, rain, and golden grain.

The
Marlin

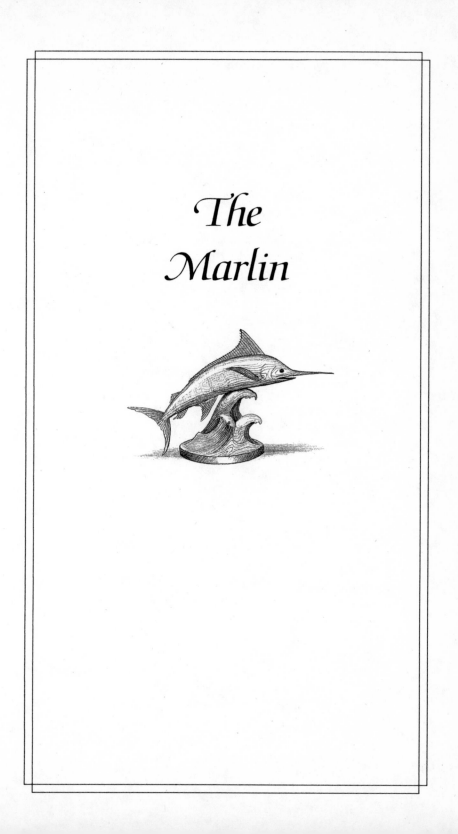

YESTERDAY IT CAME, CAREFULLY WRAPPED IN brown paper and a sturdy cardboard box...a gorgeous hand-carved, hand-polished carving of a leaping marlin. It was a thing of pure beauty, of exquisite artistry, of pulsing power shaped with loving care by the rough hands of a Mexican craftsman. Its soft smooth luster came from the gentle polishing of his children's slender fingers and pressing palms.

I have always loved wood carvings of any kind, whether as rare as this leaping swordfish shaped from the rare Ironwood of Mexico or a grizzly bear chiseled from a block of poplar. The color of the wood, the graceful lines of the grain, and the texture of the fibers are exciting and lovely to behold.

As I unwrapped the piece the winter sun streamed through the great bay window. Outside all the hills and lake lay draped in snow and ice. We were 2000 miles from the warm waters of the South Pacific, but in the square of sunlight splashed so brightly on our front room floor The

27

Marlin pulsed with light so intense that it was as if it leaped from the bright blue waves of its native habitat.

I held it gently, reverently in my hands. Its smooth polish was as slick as glass. The carver had shaped it with meticulous perfection from a rough chunk of multihued Ironwood. Its base was rugged like a storm-tossed sea. But the great swordfish arched from the waves in pure power.

The light and dark grain of the wood followed the muscled contours of the body. It flared out in flashing form on the great dorsal fin. It was a rare and gorgeous piece of primitive art that made me tremble with pure delight.

There had been quite a story behind this leaping marlin which I now held so tenderly in my warm hands. I had first seen this sort of craftsmanship in a small shop on a faraway island. But most of the work was rather rough and quite crude. I was sure if I searched long enough I would finally find a swordfish of superb design.

So I stumbled from shop to shop without much success. Then one warm evening, just as the sun set in splendor behind the swaying palms, I spotted the prize piece in a tiny shop. It was half-buried from sight by other bric-a-brac. I lifted it quietly into the light, blew the dust from its shining surface, and gazed in awe at its beauty.

Sadly, the only girl in the shop could hardly speak English. The shop owner was away, and she really did not know the proper price for the crafted piece. I decided to return the next day. It was almost a replay, except this time a different girl grinned sheepishly and taunted me by quoting an absurd price far beyond reason. I walked out in dismay.

The last morning on the island, just before my departure, in melancholy mood I decided to at least walk by the tiny shop and gaze upon this piece for one last time. To my surprise a different woman, quite pleasant, was in the shop. I asked if she was the owner. "No," she smiled, "but I am happy to help you."

Since I had given up hope of purchasing the wood carving I came without purse or wallet, so I had no money on me. And anyway I was sure the store would still ask the same outrageous price. But I was wrong... very wrong.

The pleasant lady handed me the piece to hold once more. I told her of my previous attempts to purchase it. Then she quoted me a low, low figure. She must have sensed intuitively just how deeply I admired it. I swallowed hard to hide my astonishment. Then I explained in embarrassment that I had no money with me, nor could I return, for I was due to leave in just a few minutes.

Her eyes filled with compassion. "Just give me your name and home address," she smiled softly. "I will hide this piece just for you. When you get home send me the price we agreed on, and I will ship it to you."

I was ecstatic with delight. But still I was not at all sure such a miracle could happen in our complicated world... a world of empty promises, broken contracts, and double dealing. Perhaps this would be different. At least I would trust this kindly lady on a faraway island.

When I got home a money order with a brief covering letter was sent off in quiet faith. Perhaps this purchase would work out in a unique and wonderful way... with my Father's help.

And it did!

For yesterday, in the brilliant splash of sun falling on my front-room floor, I undid the rough brown paper, and there stood The Marlin I had chosen with such care. It stood there shining in the sun, poised in power on its pedestal.

What a lovely bonus in life!
What a joy to know there are still some
simple, honest people to be trusted.
What a lift to the human spirit.

My soul began to sing, for always The Marlin will remind me there are still some precious, simple, honest people among us . . . even though they be utter strangers in faraway places.

The
Vacuum
Cleaner

*S*EVERAL WEEKS AGO THE BIG BULKY vacuum cleaner which Ursula uses with such gusto simply stopped functioning properly. We tried all the usual tricks to make it work, but the only response was a wild scream from the motor that nearly deafened both of us.

Not being a mechanical man who enjoys the challenge of fixing faulty machines, I decided to take it to some "expert." But who? Where? In which one of the numerous shops that sold and serviced vacuum cleaners?

It startled me to find so many who served the public. I had no idea vacuum cleaners comprised such an impressive part of the community. They must almost match automobiles to support so many shops. Or were vacuum cleaners notorious for breakdowns and short-lived performance?

A bit bewildered, I lifted my spirit in simple prayer, asking my Father for clear direction where to go. As my fingers ran across the yellow pages I felt drawn strongly to a shop almost next-door to where a friend works in a hardware store. I would go there.

Quietly I slipped the crippled machine into the car. I wanted it repaired as a surprise for Cheri. She would be overjoyed to find it functioning with full force the next time she tackled the carpets.

It was a mean winter morning. Ice and snow were everywhere. The car slithered to a stop in front of the shop. Then I carried in the machine like a wounded warrior, stepping ever so carefully on the ice-glazed steps. The shop was open, but not a single soul could be seen, not even at the counter.

I waited a few moments. Still no one appeared. I shuffled my cold boots, cleared my throat, and hoped help would arrive. It did! A little ragtag lady dressed in denim pants and a rough bush shirt suddenly shot out of the back of the shop. Her hair was wild and uncombed, looking as if she had just tumbled out of bed five minutes before I came.

Without even asking what the trouble was, she swept the vacuum out of my hands and signaled for me to follow her back to her workbench. Every move she made was swift, efficient, and effective.

In a matter of moments she had the balky machine apart. "It's jammed full of dirt and lint!" she remarked, whipping a twisted wire from a nail on the wall. In seconds she had freed it of all the accumulated debris around the motor. "The main drive belt is off its pulley," she grunted. Seizing it with the might of a man, she stretched it hard and replaced it where it belonged. "Just step back before I blow your head off!" she commented crisply. "This blast of air will leave it as clean as a whistle."

In seven or eight minutes she had reassembled the machine and tested how it ran. It hummed smoothly, as sweetly as when it was new. She looked at me with a glow of joyous triumph in her sparkling eyes.

"How much do I owe you?" I asked, opening up my well-worn wallet. "Not a cent," she replied. "After all, I didn't have to replace a part!" It took my breath away. Such service was last known 30 years ago—not in the

1990's. The milk of human kindness still flowed in some veins . . . golden veins full of grace.

I slipped her a handsome bill from my wallet. "Treat yourself to a fine dinner!" We parted in great goodwill.

Winter
Climb

*I*T IS ONE THING TO SPEND a winter in the far north while sheltered in the environs of a large city. It is quite another to live out in the heart of the mountains, where wind, ice, snow, sleet, and stormy weather assail you from every side. The heavy overcast of low, dark clouds; the ever-deepening snow; the moaning of the north winds— all can combine forces to make a man feel somewhat under siege.

But about mid-January there comes what we sometimes call in northern terms "The Thaw" or "Midwinter Break." Slowly the temperatures begin to moderate. Imperceptibly the snow starts to melt on the southwest slopes and sheltered spots. The cloud cover begins to break open, letting a few hours of sunlight flood the icebound landscape.

For the first time in weeks one is no longer housebound. There is no new snow to shovel. Even the home fires can be allowed to burn low. Somehow the winter siege has been lifted briefly and a man is free to head for the open spaces and a hardy winter climb on a beckoning ridge.

Three days ago it was just like that. I awoke to a dawn with open skies—a breathtaking sunrise of burnished gold and still, still air. Instinctively I knew it would be a glorious interlude of good weather and good climbing.

Swiftly I made a small lunch of sandwiches, pulled on my warm wool shirt, picked up my binoculars, and slipped into my friendly old boots. It startled me to suddenly recall that the same sturdy pair had carried me through 19 winters of snow and ice!

I headed for a remote and little-known range about 30 miles from home. It was wide-open country with rough ridges, wide valleys still wild, and great brooding spaces untouched by the progress of civilization. It was pristine territory that made my spirit roar. The last time I climbed there was some 30 years ago. I was a little over 40 then, and was thrilled to encounter my first wolverine in the remote range. What would I meet on this midwinter climb—now a man well into my seventies?

To my unbounded delight the snow slopes did not disclose a single boot mark or sign of man. They were still as virgin as the first time I had come there so long ago. This was rare indeed in our rapidly changing world. Here at least, on this remote mountain range, it was as if time stood still. And I was privileged to step into a realm as yet unmarred by man.

The winter air was brisk, not chilling; sharp, not cutting; tremendously exhilarating, clear and charged with oxygen. It astonished me how well and fit and strong my legs felt as I began the ascent of the lower levels. Everywhere were abundant deer tracks. The hoofprints of bucks, does, and fawns crisscrossed the slopes as the animals foraged for the nutritious bunch grass protruding here and there through the spotless snow.

The mountain air was even more pungent with the spicy fragrance of grey sage. I plucked several stalks of the aromatic shrubs and rubbed them briskly between my hands. The sharp perfume filled my nostrils. It was always a heady sensation that reminded me of this high desert realm: the call of the coyote and the wild wings of ravens and hawks.

Steadily I gained altitude. It thrilled me to sense the powerful push in my muscles; the strong thrust in my legs and thighs; the steady, heavy throbs of my lungs inhaling great drafts of clean mountain air; even the strong surge of oxygen-charged blood rushing freely to my liver, heart, and brain. Who, even in his most sanguine dreams, could have thought I would still be high on a northern mountain slope reveling in such joy in my seventies? And this in mid-January!

Surely my Father had endowed me with vigor beyond my years, with delight beyond my deserving, with enthusiasm beyond my expectation. He it was who made life an adventure into the twilight of my years.

Because the cold temperatures of the previous weeks had been so severe, I could see where the deer had turned to forage off the lower limbs of the fir trees. They had stripped the needles and buds from the snow-laden branches of the sheltering trees. It was a survival measure if they were to endure the rough weather still to come before spring broke the grip of ice on the snow slopes.

I pushed on steadily, astounded that the stiff exertion stimulated my spirit so splendidly. I did not seem to tire. Instead my whole being was charged with fresh energy. A superb high-altitude exhilaration engulfed me, spurred on as I was by the ever-widening horizons.

Reaching the crest of the ridge, I stood proudly on the rough outcrop of rock blown clear of snow. Orange, yellow, and grey lichens adorned the surface of the stone. The bright colors were in sharp contrast to the pure whiteness of the surrounding snow.

In that contrast lay unusual beauty, design, and delight to the eye. If I had carried my camera it would have comprised a memorable photograph. But I had purposely left the camera at home. Any imprints made by this day were to be recorded only on the medium of my memory. They would be recorded there as precious mementos of an aged mountain man alone on the ridge of his youth.

Quietly, softly, surely I swept my gaze across hundreds of square miles of upland vistas. A serene stillness enfolded the whole realm. Range upon snowy range swept away to the farthest horizon in virgin folds without a single human footprint. Valley upon valley spread out below me like a quilted covering for the lower altitudes. Not a sound stirred in the great silence. A solitary man stood alone on the summit.

It was a memorable moment suspended in time. It was an intense interlude of unusual clarity. It was a time to think very long thoughts about the beauty, wonder, and awe of winter. All were free for the taking; they needed only the sturdy determination of will and discipline of body to gain their glory.

Surely, *surely* such bounties come in hearty joy and deep delight, as winter-wrapped gifts from the generous hands of my Father. I came down off that ridge a richer man than when I awoke at dawn. This was a day He had arranged for my special satisfaction.

That night I slept the sweet sleep of a small child. Not a limb seemed to stir, not an eyelash seemed to flicker. It was as if again I had, for a lovely, brief interlude, found the fountain of youth. I felt as fresh as a youth in the springtime of life.

In His gentle, sure, and wonderful way my Father had made good His wondrous promise to me: "Who satisfieth thy mouth with good things, so that thy youth is renewed like the eagle's" (Psalm 103:5).

Such commitments are much more than mere poetic imagery. They are the dynamic, living reality that can be a vital, pulsing part of life for the person who enjoys God's companionship.

His life, His energy, His remarkable enthusiasm can come to me in a thousand ways on different days. On this midwinter climb He spoke to me in solitude;

in the pristine purity of many slopes;
in the sweet fragrance of wild sage;
in the splendor of soaring peaks against
blue skies;
in the surging strength of my own
bloodstream rushing through my veins;
in the wonder of His Word;
in the stillness of the earth;
in the intense awareness of His
presence with me.
And I was renewed!

Meat Pie
and
Shoveled
Drive

*S*OME INCIDENTS IN LIFE DROP INTO the lap of our daily experiences like gilt-wrapped gifts. They are quite unexpected, very surprising, stimulating to the spirit.

For two weeks it had snowed off and on almost every day. I was beginning to weary of shoveling snow, cleaning giant cornices of snow off the roof, knocking snow off each block of wood carried in for the heater, cleaning snow from doorways and driveways. It seemed there was no end to snow, snow, snow. I even wondered where room could be found to pile the wind-driven drifts.

Then it happened. Suddenly one day I came home gingerly through the gathering gloom to find that all the driveway, the sidewalks, and even the doorways had been shoveled clean.

Stunned, I paused momentarily in the drive. It simply seemed too good to believe. The bare pavement appeared almost unreal. The huge piles of snow heaped up on every side astonished me.

Did someone, with more strength than I, care enough to come over and do this job out of sheer goodwill and heartwarming concern? Yes, someone did, and he did it with gusto.

I learned later that it was a young man from town, ten miles away. With enormous energy and strong muscles he had moved mountains of snow on my behalf. With this one gracious act of generosity he had not only saved my aching old back, but he had broken the back of winter.

In a warm and wonderful way my spirit welled up with profound gratitude. What a lift our Father gave me through that young man's strong arms!

Then another evening the doorbell rang. I went to see who was there. Cold wind tugged at the eaves and swirled around the door. I opened it carefully to keep out the formidable frost.

Standing there all wrapped up in wool cap, mitts, and thick winter jacket stood a neighbor. His bright blue eyes sparkled above crimson cheeks. "Just brought you a wee treat," he muttered, pushing a covered basket of food toward me. "I won't come in just now—too much winter." And he was gone.

Softly I unwrapped the unexpected gift. It steamed hot and pungent and tantalizing . . . a fresh, home-baked meat pie, drawn from the oven only moments before. Beside it was a piping hot bowl of rich dark gravy. What a feast! What a banquet to nourish one's body battling midwinter ice and sleet!

No talk here about cholesterol in your arteries, or too much fat in your diet. One's whole being craved and longed for hearty food and delicious fat to fend off the onslaught of winter weather.

Every mouthful of the delicious meal was relished. Every particle of pie was consumed with contentment. Every drop of gravy was licked up with glorious delight. It was a meal that will be remembered to the end of my days.

That night I curled up like a cat and slept for nine hours solid. I had peace and rest and deep, deep joy... besides quickened faith in the gentle goodness of generous neighbors.

In this weary old world there are still some sterling souls who really do love their neighbors as they love themselves... even to meat pies and home-made gravy. Splendid fare!

Moonset

*I*T HAD BEEN ONE OF THOSE clear, still, chill winter nights. A full moon, like an orb of polished white gold, rode high in the star-studded sky. Hour by hour the temperatures settled lower and lower. The entire earth was in the death grip of Arctic cold.

Every hill, every ridge, every valley, every lake was locked in ice, shimmering white and bright under its mantle of frosty snow. A stray coyote, a dark ghost of the night, hunted for mice among the bunch grass tussocks. A grey owl on soft, silent wings floated through the dark pine trees.

All the world waited for morning.
But before dawn came, the moon must set.

Slowly, steadily, surely it sank toward the high hills to the west. As it did so its intense white light of midnight turned steadily into a golden glow.

The burnished light spread a golden sheen over the entire landscape. Most arresting was its remarkable reflection off the glare ice on the lake. Like a giant mirror made of polished glass the splendor of the moonset in the west filled the whole valley with a few moments of golden glory.

Lost in wonder, awe, and inspiration I stood alone at the window, breathless within the beauty before me. Perhaps no other person within 70 miles shared the mystery and the majesty of the moment.

I was in my 71st year—a man of the high mountains—yet this moonset was rare and lovely. It came as a special gift of grace and uplift directly from my Father's hands. What a memory!

The Woodpile

I N THIS NORTHERN MOUNTAIN VALLEY, FROST and snow
and glistening ice are part of life for about four months
in the year. From mid-November, when gusting winds
strip the last scarlet leaves from the sumac bushes, to
mid-March, when the golden-breasted meadowlarks sing
in the sage, winter is king. For even if the hills are bare
and brown, still the high ridges are white with snow. Cold
winds howl like hunting wolves, and night temperatures
drop below freezing.

To have a home that is warm and wonderful with
the redolence of burning wood it is imperative to have a
hefty pile of wood close at hand. There really is nothing
else in all the world to match the gentle, living warmth
that comes from burning wood. Each type of tree burns in
its own special way. Our sturdy Douglas fir burns with
fierce heat and long duration. The light and energy of a
hundred summer suns have been locked tightly in its rich
red fibers. The sharp crackle of cedar with its exploding
flames makes for the finest kindling in the world. The

steady heat, crimson coals, and sweet fragrance of black birch make any fire an uplift to the spirit.

At times the hauling, splitting, piling, and carrying of wood may seem an endless chore. But bit by bit I have come to see that there is a great good in these gentle yet strenuous tasks. The swing of an axe, the stooping and lifting of logs, the climbing of stairs with armloads of wood—all stretch the muscles, exercise the back and legs, strengthen the spine, and send blood surging through the body.

Each in its own way is excellent therapy.

But beyond that there is a solace of spirit to be found in feeding a wood fire. Perhaps it is the rekindling of an ancient instinct, a call back to those days when a man's survival in winter depended on a flaming fire that held the winter wolf at bay.

I am at heart still a primitive person—one of those rare people who still enjoys pitting my strength against the raw, unleashed elements of wind and storm and howling blizzards. What if the power lines go down? What if all the electric lights go out? What if the roads all drift deep with snow or are plugged shut with thundering avalanches? There is still that pile of wood that can fend off the darkest threat of the long winter nights.

That silent pile of wood is better than any insurance, superior to any hydro crews, safer than any service company in the country.

Yes, indeed, that pile of wood spells security in tangible ways that spell contentment,

and peace,
hot cups of tea,
a warm snug house,
hot meals at hand,
the gentle crackle of good cheer,
the sweet aroma of burning wood.

Modern man with all his technology cannot touch the deep longings for inner security that a rough, hand-split pile of wood can provide.

Come to think of it, even wood itself is one of my Father's choicest gifts to me as His child. Not only does it warm my home, but it also warms my body, warms my heart, warms my friends . . . and helps to keep me fit and vigorous.

Thank You, Father, for wood. Thank You for strength to swing an axe. Thank You for the sturdy muscles to lift logs and pack armloads of fragrant fuel!

Quail
Hill

QUAIL ARE NOT A NATIVE BIRD to this northern edge of the desert. They were brought here by the early pioneers, who felt sure that hardy California birds would do well in this realm of sage-brush, greasewood, and cactus. They were right, for now the tough little characters have claimed the whole country as their own.

Still, there sometimes come severe seasons and adverse weather when one wonders if they can survive. This winter was a case in point. For weeks the snow fell. It piled up deeper every day. Even on the southwest slopes, where wind and sun tend to keep the ground exposed, the snow cover became white and menacing. The birds would have a tough time finding any feed to fire their bodies.

Our hill is one of their favorite foraging grounds. The steep slopes facing the southern sun are generally bare. Here amid the rabbitbrush and greasewood thickets the sturdy birds come to forage. But this winter it was different, and for weeks I never saw a single quail. Perhaps the wicked, cold nights with wind chill down to

32 degrees below zero had wiped them out, chilled to the bone and starved to mere skeletons.

Then one sunny morning about ten days ago I heard the distinct, challenging call of a male bird. Despite the worst of snow and ice and frost at least this doughty chap defied the elements. A strange, stirring surge of hope welled up within me. Perhaps a few stragglers would survive.

It was a peculiar, frail, faltering bit of faith that believed somehow the wild ones would make it through the winter storms. Maybe, just maybe!

Then two days ago a wonderful, warm, midwinter thaw settled softly into our valley. Gently the snow began to go. Dark patches of earth and grass and gravel were interspersed with the snow. The overcast opened up and a flood of golden sunshine warmed the land.

I pulled on boots, slipped into a jacket, and headed into the hills for a brisk climb. As I came home an hour later I stopped dead-still in my tracks. There, right beside my house, on a sun-splashed patch of gravel, scurried a lively covey of quail. There were at least 30 of the handsome birds, all fluffed up, eagerly picking up gravel and plucking the last berries from an ornamental shrub growing against the wall.

The birds were in peak condition. Not one appeared weak, winter-worn, or malnourished. They darted about and strutted their stuff with all the energy and elegance so typical of this species. My spirit soared. "You tough little characters, you made it after all!" The words, though muttered silently to myself in pure delight, seemed to trigger an instant response in the flock: "We'll show you, boss!" In à spontaneous, explosive thunder of wings they all took flight. Swiftly, deftly, surely they sailed over the hill to alight in formation on the open slopes below.

I was glad, glad, glad! Thrilled to the depths with sheer joy to see my friends in such fine form. I rushed into the house to share the good news with Cheri.

Our eyes met in mutual good cheer. She too had already seen them. We laughed with pleasure. Spring could not be far away. And quail would fill our world again. Yes, our Father cared for quail as well.

The Manuscript

*T*HE BOOK HAD TAKEN MONTHS AND months to write. Morning after morning, long before dawn, I had compiled the work with meticulous care. It was all handwritten, using an old-fashioned fountain pen, as had been my custom for some 40 years. And this particular book would be the fortieth compiled under my name.

Now the pressing question was, Who will type this manuscript? Out of a sense of nostalgia I wrote to a secretary on the coast who had done a book for me some 20 years ago. She replied at once that, though well-advanced in years, she felt equal to the challenge and would take it on when we came to the coast in winter.

As it turned out, that was not to be. Fierce winter storms, deep snow, and pipe-bursting cold made it imperative to stay home and stoke our fires. So a second time the search was on for a skilled secretary. It was not an easy quest. Not everyone can read my writing. And even when they can, I insist that the work be well-nigh word perfect to satisfy my publishers.

Quietly I entreated my Father to bring someone to mind who would be able to suggest a suitable secretary. The next morning I felt prompted to call a longtime friend. To my unbounded delight she immediately offered to do the work herself. It startled me to find her so enthusiastic for the project. At the same time I knew assuredly it was in the most capable hands.

Without delay I placed the work in her care, and then relaxed in the knowledge that all was well.

Or was it?

Neither one of us dreamed just then what a supreme challenge and test of endurance this would be. It is often fortunate in life that we do not know what lies ahead of us on the path. It is a mercy from our Father that He gives us sufficient faith to trust Him for each unknown step we take, just one day at a time.

The dear lady, skilled and proficient in her profession, encountered one setback after another—not because of any fault on her part, but rather because the equipment she worked with chose to break down again and again. One obstacle after another would arise to thwart her progress. It demanded incredible endurance and unflinching fortitude to carry on the project.

I was deeply concerned for her setbacks. It was no simple thing to overcome one high hurdle after another. What would be the final outcome?

Then one balmy afternoon the doorbell rang. There she stood, face radiant, eyes shining with triumph. In her hands she held the fully completed work, done with meticulous care and unflinching precision.

My whole being surged with unbounded delight. What pure joy poured through my spirit! Endurance had prevailed. Faith had overcome. Goodwill had triumphed over every adversity. In gratitude I gave her a hearty hug. This project had been more than a test of professional expertise; it had also been a resounding victory for those who truly trust in God.

The beautiful bonus in all of this was the great spiritual impetus which the work had given this dear lady. From it she was fortified in her own faith, quickened to devote herself even more fully to Christ.

He makes all things turn out for our final good!

The Quiet Place

*T*HOSE OF US WHO, EITHER BECAUSE of advanced age or the constrictions of winter weather, must spend much of our time indoors need a quiet place in the home. It does not have to be elaborate, but it must be a serene spot set apart from the main part of the house—a place where the incessant demands of the telephone or the raucous intrusion of the television or the clatter of the kitchen do not dominate the domestic scene.

Peace and privacy are becoming precious elements in our crowded, noisy world. Each of us needs a quiet place where we can withdraw a bit from our frantic way of life to find repose in solitude. We need time to be alone, to give our Father a chance to commune with us and we with Him. We need moments of stillness to think quietly, to reminisce gently, to relish the moment with a good book or some superb music.

When first I was shown through this home, high on a hill, only the upstairs had been fully finished.

The lower floor, though roughed in, was far from complete. But its ambience attracted me at once. Because of its location on a high promontory, even the downstairs rooms were high above ground level. They had beautiful, big, full-sized windows and even a massive glass door that looked out over the blue lake below and the snowcapped ranges beyond.

To reach the rooms downstairs one descended down a unique spiral staircase of exquisite design. Fortunately the steps and walls were all fully carpeted so that it was virtually a soundproof entrance to the lower level. Happily, too, this helped to reduce the injuries when I fell down the stairs one dark night.

Ursula was awakened from a deep sleep by the rumble and roar of my rapid descent. But, assuming it was just another thunderstorm in the valley, she happily rolled over and went on sleeping.

The serious question which had to be answered was not the matter of minor accidents like this, but rather how to turn the downstairs into a quiet place—a true retreat, not just where *I* could go to study and write and meditate, but others could as well. I can do rough carpentry, but I am not a skilled craftsman. And the costs of completion could be daunting. So for the better part of several years all I did was dream about the possibilities. Yes, I even hoped that perhaps someday I could have a private office down there.

Then one gentle day last autumn, when the last leaves were falling from the wind-tossed trees, a young couple came to visit us. He was a first-class carpenter who had done superb work for me in our tiny cottage at Still Waters. Without any prompting from us he suddenly spoke up calmly and said, "I feel constrained to come over here and finish up your basement. If you supply the materials I will do all the work!" I was exhilarated, excited, jubilant with joy.

To our unbounded delight the whole job was done with meticulous precision. No pains were spared. If ever there was a "labor of love and concern," this was it, executed with fun, laughter, and good cheer.

In such gracious, generous, gentle ways our Father brings our dreams to life, our hopes to reality, and our hearts to overflowing gratitude. He does this through His own dear people.

This morning I am writing these lines in the quiet place.

Tonight I will teach an eager Bible class in this place.

All is well!

Good
Health

*F*OR MUCH OF MY LIFE ILLNESS was an integral part of living. I grew up in a region of East Africa where malaria, dysentery, typhoid, and other tropical diseases were abundant. Most people, both native and European, suffered from these afflictions. Nor was I exempt. For years and years I struggled with recurring attacks of malaria.

Even well into my sixties it seemed my body did battle with bacterial infections and various viruses picked up from other people. One day, in a quiet hour of reflection, I went over the long list of ailments I had endured. It astonished me to realize that some 36 different disorders had assailed my body during the years it housed me.

Yet, strange as it may sound, not a single day had ever been spent in a hospital. Nor, apart from having my tonsils removed as a small tot, had a surgeon's scalpel ever touched me. For healing and restoration of health I had relied for the most part on rest, nourishing food, loving home care, and a quiet trust in Christ, my dearest Friend and finest Physician.

But more astonishing than all of this has been the gradual, steady renewal of my strength and vitality as an older man. Not that I claim to possess the vigor and stamina of a young man. I do not. But I do enjoy a level of well-being I never dreamed possible earlier in life.

I awake early, refreshed and invigorated by deep sleep. I have a zest for life and an eagerness to work well.

A level of wholesome well-being, of strong purpose and vitality, pervades my whole being. It surges through my body. It pulses in my veins. Though more than 70 summers have come and gone, I have the sweet sensation of a youth in the springtime of life.

For me that lovely passage in Psalm 103:5 is a powerful reality from the Lord: "Who satisfieth thy mouth with good things, so that thy youth is renewed like the eagle's."

In humility, wonder, awe, and genuine gratitude I bow myself before Him and give thanks for good health. It is one of His supreme and special gifts imparted to me in my twilight years.

If I may be allowed to do so here, I wish to give personal thanks to Christ Himself for this gracious bounty. For it is only in recent times that I have calmly accepted His body, His life, His very blood in communion as His great gift to me. In simple, quiet, unflinching faith I take His dynamic body and His purifying lifeblood to be my portion as well. Not just for moral, spiritual cleansing and restoration, but also for mental and physical redemption and rejuvenation.

This is a private, intimate interaction between the Living Christ and myself. It is an act of calm confidence in His capacity to care for me, to sustain me in wholesomeness, to empower me to be a healthy, whole person who honors Him . . . in body, soul, and spirit.

As He daily empowers me with His well-being, in turn it is possible to accomplish those duties He entrusts to me with vigor, enthusiasm, and good cheer. What an adventure with Him!

Promise
of
Spring

*T*WO DAYS AGO THAT FIRST SONG of a meadowlark floated across the grass glades of the rolling hills below our house. It was pure, and clear, and stirring. That unmistakable song with its clear, flowing, liquid notes stirs me to the depths, for it spells *spring*!

The day was warm, still, and pulsing with the promise of new life. We live on the northern edge of the great Sonora Desert, a dry and arid region extending all across eastern Washington, Oregon, Utah, Arizona, and California deep into Mexico. Across this vast expanse of windblown benches, grey sage, lava rock, and rolling rangeland the bursting songs of meadowlarks reach for the open, sun-filled skies. Ten thousand such songs poured out in exultation never even reach a human ear nor move a human heart. But up here, in the deep desert valley that runs like a terminal tentacle into the heart of our British Columbian hills, the meadowlark songs are special.

They echo off the rock walls of the canyons. They waft across the lakes. They flow over the brown hills dotted with ponderosa pines. They are picked up by people like myself who yearn for the advent of spring and the end of winter.

So I was elated when the meadowlarks sang. Surely spring had come. The sun seemed so warm, the air so balmy, the day so stimulating. I took off my shirt and let the warm rays enfold my arms, my back, my chest.

Yes, spring was here. I was sure! No more need to split wood, to lay fires, to shovel snow, to dread black ice on the roads. Or was there?

Suddenly yesterday morning the wind shifted. Gusts of cold air from the Arctic began to blow down from the north. They came with such force as to create giant swells in the lake that lifted the melting ice, breaking it into fractured, floating slabs. I had never seen this happen before. I did not realize that great thin sheets of ice could actually bend and roll and undulate under wind pressure.

With the wind came first of all a few random flurries of snow. The first flakes were like forerunners, falling from the overcast in random, wild confusion. As soon as they touched the ground they were gone, turned to droplets of moisture by the warm soil, heated by the sun the day before.

But by noon all of that white confusion had turned into a formidable "whiteout." A solid stream of snow, power-driven by the northern gale, filled our valley. The pervading whiteness also brought a deepening darkness. The heavy overcast and driving snow blocked out the sun, blocked out the view, and blocked out the birds.

Not a single bird song could be heard!

The snow began to cover the hills, the grass, the trees, the shrubs. Slowly but surely all the earth was etched only in black and white. A deathlike stillness settled over the scene.

Within my spirit a profound pain and burning concern pulled at my consciousness for the birds. Some had flown thousands of miles to find this spot in the sun. Now it was in the grim grip of ice and snow and frost.

The promise of spring had lured them into mortal peril and the danger of death.

Life is often like that for each of us.

We have known those times when hope filled our hearts and joy spilled from us in glorious songs. Then suddenly, all unawares, the spring days were filled with sadness.

Still, in life, things are not always as they appear. Beneath and behind the storms of adversity there stands in the shadow of our sorrow the loving, caring person of our Father. He too knows all about the meadowlarks caught in a spring storm. He cares for the robins and song sparrows sheltering in the ice-sheathed trees. He is aware of the ospreys not able to fish in the ice-choked lake.

And because He cares, these brave birds of warm blood, sturdy sinews, and bright eyes will find a way to survive. The spring storm will not destroy them. The promise of spring will prevail.

In a few days there will be a break in the clouds. Patches of blue sky will appear in the overcast. Sunshine will warm the earth again. The sound, so gentle, of melting snow and dripping water will caress the countryside. Buds will burst open; green grass will glow on the south slopes; brown soil will supplant the snow.

> Spring will be here.
> The sun will surpass
> the snow.

> And meadowlarks will
> sing in the sagebrush
> hills again.

They did! With delight and exuberance.

My
Friend

*H*E IS JUST THE SORT OF man many would choose as a special friend. He lives alone amid a tangle of books, paintings, bits of woodland roots, and odds and ends of song sheets. The latter lie scattered on his sofa and strewn about his front room.

But he is a man with a happy heart.
He is one with a ready smile and a hearty
chuckle.
He is aglow with goodwill, filled with
great good cheer.

He is always eager to see me, glad to welcome me into the warmth of his home. He enfolds me in a great bear hug, his eyes shining with pure pleasure.

There are deep bonds between us, forged from our common love and loyalty to Christ. We speak much of our Master when we are together. We share the pure joy and deep delight we find in His company. We tell often of His glorious grace and magnificent mercy to us. We relish the joy of recounting our Father's faithfulness to us as His sons.

There flows between us a lovely mirth of great exhilaration. We laugh together until tears course down our cheeks. We bask in the open and unabashed pleasure of each other's company.

We always pray together. Not long complicated prayers, but short, sincere entreaties for people in need, but more specifically for each other. We can do this in simplicity, in sincerity.

Because he is my friend.

A very special gift from God!

First
Buttercup

                    So tiny!
                        So brilliant!
                            So full of good cheer!
                                Spring is surely here.

I WAS CLIMBING A STEEP SLOPE OF land just below the
house. There in a sheltered spot, protected by
ponderosa pines that broke the north wind, the solitary
little plant burst into bloom, first of the season.

I had almost stepped on it, unseen. For it was half-
hidden among the brown duff of fallen pine needles and
last year's old growth grass. Happily my boot missed it by

inches. And when I saw its golden glory, not much more than a small thimble cup of shining yellow, I paused in mid-stride.

At once all my thoughts turned to spring, to warm sunshine, to ten thousand other wild blossoms that would explode into color across our tawny hills. But it took only one tiny buttercup, crouched close to the soil, to turn all my attention to the hope, joy, and abundant life that spring can bring.

Yes, one tiny plant flowering in a realm of apparent desolation—of brown needles, brown grass, brown earth, all so drab and sere—had stopped me in my tracks. Its butter-yellow petals soft as satin, smooth as silk, caught the sunlight falling on them to reflect its splendor for a fleeting second to a passing person.

In that moment my mind was transformed, my spirit soared, great good cheer welled up within. All because a solitary little buttercup bloomed on a bare hill.

I wonder . . . I wonder . . . I wonder.

Does my little life—so common, so plain, so simple—reflect the glory of my sun, the Living Lord? Does it arrest those who pass me on the dusty path of life?

The
Pastoral
Painting

*T*HERE ARE MOMENTS IN LIFE THAT slip softly into our experience unannounced, but with deep delight and joy beyond words. They are startling surprises, poignant and powerful, filled with pure pleasure. I call them "my Father's beautiful bonuses."

Last Saturday one of these came my way when we visited friends who are preparing to move into a much smaller home than the one they now occupy. As is common with all of us, such moves call for drastic decisions. Furniture and ornaments and surplus possessions simply have to be sorted out, sold, or discarded.

In the midst of their move Barbara had come across a watercolor piece of great vintage. It had been in her family for years. But now the gilt frame was damaged and the pastoral scene of a small flock of sheep in a rural setting seemed dated. It was hardly suitable for a sharp, modern condominium. Yet in her loving way she set it aside for me, because of my enduring fondness for country life and livestock.

Gently and tenderly she placed the painting in my

hands. For an instant my old heart almost skipped a sturdy beat or two. For, despite the damaged frame, the ancient padding on the back, and the apparent antiquity of the piece, I held in my rough hands a great treasure. The warm tones of the work appealed to me at once.

They were so true to life, so typical of an unadorned rural scene. The great expanse of brooding sky, with rain in the offing; the rugged old windblown pines leaning away from the wind; the thickets of brambles, with the sheep beyond—all rang true!

The artist, a Scot named Murray Thompson, was no amateur or apprentice. The balance of his composition is superb. The interaction of his colors is that of a master craftsman. The skill of his brushwork is exquisite. Every aspect of the work is authentic, appealing, and artistically reassuring.

Carefully, tenderly, I placed the painting in the back of the car and brought it home with the excitement of a small boy. The next day I searched the stores to find a small bottle of antique gold paint with which to restore the damaged frame. It did a lovely renewal. I polished the glass, and then, with racing pulse, hung the piece in my office in full view of my desk.

It was a perfect place to hang it.

The warm light from the great window fell on it with added splendor. The whole scene of trees, sky, stream, shrubs, and sheep came to life. And all this beauty was embellished by the refurbished golden frame.

Here was a treasure that slipped softly into my life without my foreknowledge ... like a glorious gift prepared in loving care to bring special joy and rich contentment. The painting brings an aura of remarkable peace and tranquility into the room. There is a lovely sense of serenity and stillness to the scene. Above all it is a gesture of goodwill and loving generosity.

It is a gentle reminder that in the ebb and flow of life between friends, some of the most simple gestures can also be some of the grandest. Our Father has His way of filling our days with pure delight through the warm hearts of those who care ... yes ... who care sincerely.

The
Sonata

*T*HE WORD "SONATA" IMMEDIATELY CONJURES UP before our minds the idea of exquisite music and melodious harmonies. It seemed to me, when first I heard it used in connection with cars, an unusual name for an automobile built of nuts, bolts, panels of steel, and rubber tires. And so I was determined to see one for myself, and, if possible, test-drive it on the road.

As soon as the first shipment of these automobiles came to town, Ursula and I went down to the Hyundai dealer to see the Sonatas. We already owned a little Hyundai Pony, and it had proved to be a sturdy, reliable, no-nonsense car that gave us excellent economy with a minimum of maintenance. If this newer, larger car from the same company was equally satisfactory we would be glad to own one.

Much to my delight, the dealer was not only happy to let us test-drive the Sonata, but also presented me with a handsome wristwatch for being one of the first customers to do so. That watch, by the way, I still wear every day, and it was given to me four years ago. It keeps perfect time and never needs to be wound. If the car was of equal quality it would be a marvelous piece of mechanical engineering.

We liked the car the day we drove it. The Mitsubishi motor, built in Japan, gave spirited performance with maximum economy. The interior of the car was exceedingly spacious, a most attractive feature for a man with my long legs. The vehicle was quiet to drive, smooth in its ride, and well-equipped with those features that make an automobile a pleasure to handle.

Only the price seemed prohibitive . . . a bit beyond our budget.

We are patient people, and we could wait awhile. Perhaps down the road a ways a chance would come to own a Sonata at a less drastic cost. One great lesson some 70 years of living have taught me is "All good things come to those who wait!"—and especially to those prepared to await God's good time and place and provision.

Three years rolled by without us getting any closer to owning a Sonata. Then suddenly a year ago Ursula felt urged to go and have another look. She rushed home all excited, flushed, and joyous. There was a special two-tone model in town that she was sure was just for us. With mounting enthusiasm I went back with her to the dealer to have a look. To be sure, she had indeed found a handsome car. But the moment I looked inside, my spirit sank in dismay. It was not a new vehicle. It had been pre-owned and driven hard. I simply was not interested.

The saleslady who had shown Ursula the car was called Marguerite. She was a pleasant person, very knowledgeable about the Sonata, and rather saddened by our decision not to purchase the car Ursula liked so well. Still, she was very courteous, kind, and understanding. She promised to keep in touch, in the event a special buy came up in a Sonata suited to our needs.

Almost another year passed. In the meantime I had sold my truck and in an impulsive, unwise move purchased a small car that was in truth a "lemon." Most of the vehicles I ever owned have served me well over long spans of time. For the first time in my life I was now stuck with a "bucket of bolts." What was I to do? We looked for some way out, but nothing seemed to open up. Finally one morning, after earnest prayer about the car, I concluded I would simply have to live with my mistake— "the lemon."

In that significant, spiritual act of just quietly accepting the fact that I was willing to live with "the lemon," the supernatural energy of my Father's loving concern was released in my dilemma. No longer did I fight against the futility of owning this wretched car. In the acceptance there came inner calm and the still assurance that all would be well. My part was to wait . . . not to fret and worry.

Hardly an hour had elapsed when the phone rang. To my utter astonishment it was Marguerite on the line. In her cordial, gentle manner she reminded me that we had looked at the Sonata a year ago. Would we still be interested? Her company had just put one of the cars on sale at a drastic discount.

I replied that we were indeed. The difficulty was that I was stuck with "a bucket of bolts" and could see no way to retrieve my mistake. With genuine concern and deep compassion she urged me to come down and see the Sonata. She was sure she could help.

When we walked into her sales lot there stood a handsome, regal Sonata shining in all its splendor. In the window of the car was a huge sign with the words "CAPTAIN'S SPECIAL, TODAY $10,900." It took my breath away. Surely a car of this caliber could not be purchased at this low price in this part of the country! There must be a catch.

But there was not!

It was a brand-new automobile, equipped exactly as we wished, at a modest price we were prepared to pay.

But what about the "bucket of bolts"? In her own gracious, genial manner Marguerite took it off our hands.

And two days later I drove home with the car of my dreams and a singing heart. Time and travel have confirmed that the Sonata lives up to its name. It is a song to own, a delight to drive, another melody in life.

Every time I get into the car, there floods over me an overwhelming outflow of gratitude to my Father for His provision . . . for His love . . . for His happy care. This car has brought us enormous contentment and great fun. It is a driver's car in the truest sense of that phrase. It just loves to literally soar down the road with effortless ease. It travels in remarkable smoothness and silence so we can relax and converse without raising our voices. Perhaps most astonishing, it averages well over 40 miles per gallon on country driving.

All of this is most remarkable when I recall that four years ago when I first drove a Sonata, they were priced at 3000 dollars more than what I paid for this one.

Such are the ways of God my Father, even in such mundane matters as buying a car of great quality and selling a lowly "lemon."

And thank you, too, Marguerite, for all your gentle care and kindness. Little wonder you are the top salesperson in your company!

Spring Ramble

*S*PRING IN THE FAR NORTH IS a peculiar season of powerful tugs and pulls within the human spirit. There surges through the senses a compelling passion to get out and go . . . to break free from the long confinement of winter . . . to roam at random. This primal urge is sometimes called "spring fever" or at other times "March madness."

Yesterday morning I was gripped by this inner restlessness. I knew from long experience that a vigorous ramble in the high country would cure the condition. But I scarcely expected such a memorable day.

Quickly I packed a hearty bag of sandwiches, slipped into old hiking gear, and put camera and binoculars in my pockets. It is only about 20 minutes from our door to the Bighorn winter range south of us. Soon I was on the slopes that led up to giant grey and brown cliffs above.

I began to climb steadily through the dense stands of grey sage, greasewood and low cactus. It was about 12 years since I had scaled these high ridges the last time. I

wondered if my strength was up to it again. I would give
it a try!

In a matter of a few minutes I spotted a small band
of half-a-dozen ewes lying among the rocks on one of their
lofty lookouts. They were watching me climb. At once the
old thrill of making a careful stalk swept through me. I
would see what the day would bring. How close could I
come to the crafty mountain climbers?

It was a cool morning. Broken clouds drifted across
the sun, so climbing came easy. I was surprised at how
steadily my legs carried me up the steep slopes. And the
higher I climbed the more readily my heart met the challenge. With increased altitude ever-wider vistas spread out
below me. Now the lake came into full view, lying flat
like a map. I scanned it with my binoculars and rejoiced to
see 22 wild swans feeding in the shallows where the river
flowed into its basin. A few years ago only two or three
swans were ever seen here. So their numbers are
increasing at last! That was such a heartening thought.

For a few minutes I lay softly on a mossy outcrop
of granite. My relaxed form put the sheep at ease. They
began to feed on the tender new grass sprouting from the
thin pockets of soil wedged among the cliffs. One was
lame with an injured foreleg. She rested often, keeping a
wary eye on me.

A pair of majestic golden eagles swept along the
crest of the cliffs. No doubt they were a mating pair
returning north to rear their brood on some remote
mountain crag. The sight of eagles soaring against the
sky always reassures me that there is still the spirit of the
wilderness at work in our crowded world. Their great
grace and powerful presence alert me to the wonder of
the wild places. In their swift passing my spirit, too, is
uplifted and I give thanks for the special joy of sharing
their upland realm.

I decided to swing around the edge of a rough
ridge and stalk the sheep downwind. The strategy worked
well. Within an hour I stood only about 50 yards from

them. They were surprised to see me at their own altitude. Like sentinels they stood at attention on the highest rock in order to be sure I intended no harm. As is my custom, I called to them in low tones. Hearing my voice, they relaxed their vigil and went off to feed again.

I followed them softly, glad to be in their company. A band of wild ewes and one elderly man high on the cliffs seemed so right on this early spring day.

The hazy sun spilled spring warmth into the deep valley below me. It was exhilarating to sweep my eyes over the broken ridges and tumbled terrain that stretched away to the snow-mantled horizon. A man like myself, a son of the wilds, needed this wide, wild vista to soothe his soul and set his spirit singing. A profound, rich inner peace pervaded my whole person. A surge of deep gratitude welled up within me for the undiminished joy and delight I found in the high country. What a lovely gift from my Father above!

The ewes began to work their way up and across ever-higher ridges. I stayed with them. I had not been this high on these cliffs for years. What a thrill! I came across the scattered feathers of a raven. Picking up one of the black, shining blades I tucked it under the headband of my old felt Stetson. Perhaps a bobcat had found the hapless bird on this high place and treated himself to a banquet. Not even a shred of a single bone remained.

A few steps further on I almost trod on a sturdy mountain cottontail. These rabbits are usually quite rare in the high country. He must have had more than the usual measure of courage to survive on these stern cliffs. But broken rock offered plenty of shelter. In mere seconds he was hidden from view. I could only wish him well.

Above me, on the very crest of the ridge, I spotted a stunted, windblown pine of great beauty growing out of a crevice in solid stone. I determined to reach it even if it took the rest of the afternoon. And I did! It proved to be a tree of remarkable character. By the girth of its gnarled and twisted trunk I knew it had clung to that rock for at least a hundred years. Its wind-bent branches, tossed by ten thousand storms, were only about 15 feet in length. It was a natural bonsai.

I stood quietly in its presence, deeply touched by its unusual grace and exquisite beauty. Out of great trials and a harsh environment had come a tree of utter loveliness. I wondered to myself if this could possibly be true in some small way of my own tough character. Silently I sighed a brief prayer of entreaty that it might be so in order to inspire others. Perhaps someone, someday, would pause and be glad that he had encountered me on the trail he tramped across a lonely life.

Leaving the lovely pine, I began my descent down the mountain. It had been such a satisfying scramble. The sun settled behind a cloud bank to the west. Cool air flowed down the slopes and I was glad to head for home.

As if in a parting salute, seven ravens swept over the ridge in their noisy, ragged, tumbled flight. There should have been eight. The one missing from the four pairs had provided a banquet for a bobcat. But that was the way of the wilds—yes, for all of us: here today, gone tomorrow. So, best to enjoy the day and relish the moment. There simply is no rerun, no replay!

The final delicate finale to this lovely interlude came when a pair of chukar partridges crowded my path. I had heard their plaintive cries on the cliffs, but they are wary birds, fleet of foot and wing. Yet now this mating pair, adorned in all the full glory of their breeding plumage, paused beneath a giant ponderosa pine. There they stood in full view, more charming than any painting. I was transfixed. This was a first for me! What a thrill.

It had been an unforgettable spring scramble. I would never forget it. Such are my Father's bounties, bestowed in love and care upon His wandering child.

As I rode home softly the highlights of the day passed across my memory in vivid succession. Each was a unique cameo of pure pleasure that would be a treasure for years to come. I was a man much, much richer than when I started out on my spring ramble that morning—all because, in His kindness, God my Father had designed my life to find so much delight in a single day.

I reflected further, and recalled clearly the time some 30 years ago when first I came to live in this wild and tumbled mountain valley. The first flood of new settlers was moving into the region buying up land, building houses, starting businesses. Few of them seemed to care about preserving native wildlife of the region. But I did! I knew full well that unless steps were taken to set aside wild areas as nature preserves and wildlife sanctuaries, even a remnant could not survive the relentless onslaught of our contemporary civilization.

And so I pled with the government agencies to set aside wildlife preserves. I wrote passionate articles and whole books arousing public interest in resource conservation. I gave endless illustrated lectures and private petitions on behalf of my wild friends of hoof, wing, and paw. Slowly but steadily the effort, like that of a prophet crying in the wilderness, met with public and private response. Thousands and thousands of acres of wild terrain were preserved for wildlife use. And today vigorous and expanding populations of animals and birds abound where only a few lived so precariously before. The very range on which I hiked this day was now home to more than 2000 bighorn sheep. In short, a man truly does harvest what he plants in life. My youthful years spent so ardently in conservation now paid back abundant rewards and precious interludes in my twilight years. I am richly repaid!

The Fortieth Book

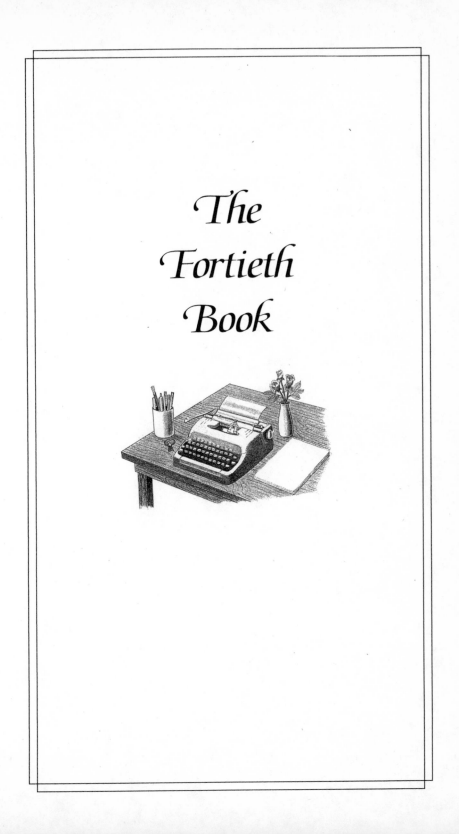

*W*HEN I WAS A SMALL BOY, growing up on a remote and wild frontier station in Kenya, some of my most impressive interludes were those hours spent alone reading great books. I had no brothers or sisters with whom to play or engage in happy adventures. And the primitive African youngsters with whom I romped occasionally were wild as the wind, untaught, untrained in any of the academic accomplishments.

Mother taught me to read at a very early age. Dad, for his part, chose excellent books for me to enjoy. They were books of great adventure, true life, noble conduct, and great outdoor enthusiasm. These volumes became my constant companions, read and reread in the solitude of my tiny room upstairs under the eaves.

I dreamed then of one day having similar great adventures. I could envision sharing them with others in books I wrote. And, I hoped sincerely, they would be as inspiring as those I read as a lad.

As with so many of the dreams which God Himself gave me across the years, this one was to come true.

After years and years of relentless writing and, it seemed, equally relentless rejections from editors and publishers, my writing began to be accepted.

It astonished me how, once the intransigence of the publishers was overcome, the readers showed so much enthusiasm for my work. Letters of gratitude came from all over the globe, especially from ordinary laypeople who appreciated the plain and simple, yet enthusiastic, manner in which I wrote. Across the years I not only wrote books but also magazine articles, regular newspaper columns, and special essays. At first it seemed my health was so frail that I would live to see only 20 books published. But in His generous compassion and kindly care my Father God restored my strength, renewed my health, and enabled me to actually see some 40 books published.

The last of these was accepted for publication only a short time ago. It was entitled simply *God Is My Delight*, and is a true statement of the profound joy that I find in Him.

The unusual and stirring aspect of this work is the impact it has already had on those who have read it. The lady who typed it was touched deeply. She wrote me a moving letter to say how profoundly God's Spirit had spoken to her from its pages.

Just a week ago this morning the managing editor who is in charge of its production told me that he had not been so excited over a book for years and years. Christ has used it in his life to inspire him with a stirring inspiration of spirit!

All of this is heartening encouragement for a man well into the twilight of life. Surely, surely the promises given to me by my Father have been honored with dignity. I stand before Him humble in heart yet jubilant with joy.

His commitments to me have been carried out with absolute credibility, just as they were carried out to His stalwarts of ancient times. His word has not altered: ''Be strong and of good courage. Be not afraid, neither be thou dismayed. For the Lord thy God is with thee whither-soever thou goest" (Joshua 1:9).

That, exactly, is what He has done!

His name be magnified!

Touched
by the
Master

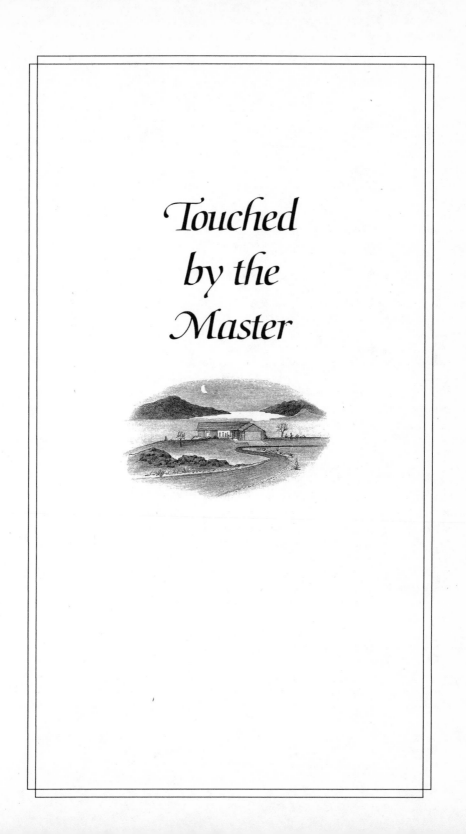

*T*HE "QUIET PLACE," MUCH TO MY commingled joy and astonishment, has proved to be a spot where all sorts of people have come to meet Christ. When we began the first Bible studies there, only three days after its completion, we told only about 12 couples about it. But to our amazement, by the second week some 50 people had packed into the place each night.

The group were of all ages, ranging from young people in their late teens to elderly octogenarians. One thing they all had in common was an eager desire to meet the Master and understand His words for them. To my unbounded delight, about half the number were men and boys.

Parking near our place is limited. So most of them had to leave their vehicles about half a block up the hill, parked over the broad shoulders of the main road. Besides this they had to walk down the hill in the dark, using flashlights to find their way. But still they came, chattering excitedly, eager to learn what the Lord had to say.

The sessions were long, often lasting two full hours, with only a five-minute break midway so they could get a drink of water, suck some sweets Ursula passed around, and stretch their legs. Yet the study was full of serious discussions, searching questions, and bright illumination of spiritual truth. Night after night God's Gracious Spirit had spoken clearly to someone.

Last Tuesday evening, after the session, a fine young man in his twenties came to me. "It is in this place that I have had a firsthand encounter with the Living Christ." A few moments later a middle-aged mother came to me, her eyes brimming with tears of joy and gratitude. "Tonight at last I can see and understand why our Father deals with me as He does. And now I am at peace!"

Such moments make these hours precious and pure. The Master, in utter fidelity and concern for the fallen and the forlorn, has come and touched them. He has healed the wounded spirits; He has filled them with the joy and exhilaration of His presence; He has dispelled their doubts and given them His deep, quiet love in place of their dark despair.

How kind and gracious He is!

He has turned our "Quiet Place" into His own special trysting place with those who will respond to His overtures of compassion.

Men and women in the simple, humble, quiet sanctuary of our home have come to know Christ. In that knowing they have entered into everlasting life.

His name be honored!

What a special silver lining amid the dark clouds of our corrupt and crass culture!

Roadside Reflections

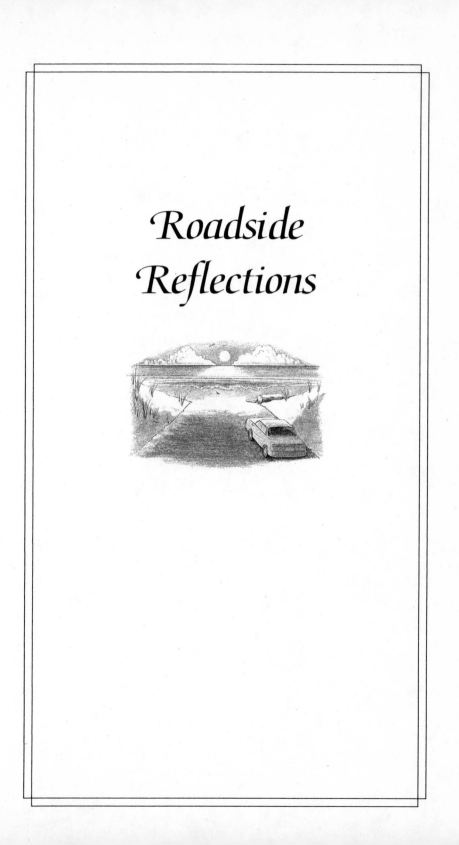

*L*AST WEEK WAS THE FIRST CHANCE in months for us to take a little trip down to the sea. A severe and stormy winter had kept us somewhat confined, close to home, amid our snow-shrouded mountains. Winter weather of unusual ferocity had made travel through our high mountain passes hazardous. Heavy snows, dangerous avalanches, icy highways, raging rivers, flooded roads, and dread winter fog had all made driving very dangerous.

But steadily, softly, spring returned to the mountains. Then finally a day was set for our departure. We left just as the sun rose over the ranges to the east. A strange, compelling excitement gripped me as we climbed over the first pass and descended into the gorgeous, rugged valley of the Similkameen River. Almost at once we began to spot the shaggy white forms of wild mountain goats on the gaunt granite cliffs above us. Each nanny in its own secluded, rock-ribbed bit of terrain was awaiting the spring arrival of its kid. Only those of us

who climbed in this rugged country were fully aware of
the drama on the cliffs.

In the quiet inner sanctum of my own spirit I
reflected on the daunting climbs I had done in this area.
A flood of warmth and reassuring memories swept
through my soul. Those had been testing interludes in
which my strength and stamina had been pitted against
the soaring ridges. My Father has given me endurance to
push on, to prevail, and to return safely with remarkable
pictures of wildlife in this high country.

But beyond even that I came back with the resolve
that some of this remarkable region should become a
splendid wilderness park. By unflinching zeal and
persistent prodding of the government this was achieved.
And today "The Cathedral Mountain Park" just a few
short miles from these goats was established as a wildlife
sanctuary for all my wild friends of hoof, wing, and paw.

We climbed steadily in our Sonata, approaching the
receding snowline at the higher elevation of the summit.
To our delight there were random bands of mule deer
feeding among the ponderosa pines. They relished every
fresh blade of green grass that pushed up from the freshly
warmed soil on the south slopes. To my surprise and joy
most of the deer appeared in healthy, robust condition.
This despite the deep snows and unusually cold temperatures of the long winter. Again their numbers would be
replenished and the race would flourish in these forests.
Humbly I bowed my heart and gave sincere thanks for
their strong survival.

At the top of the highest pass, deep snow still
blanketed the mountains. It lay over the land in depths up
to ten feet. A fresh fall two days before still clung to the
trees, the shrubs, the cliffs, the rocks. We drove through a
veritable wonderland dressed in bold black-and-white
colors. The brilliance of the new fallen snow contrasted
sharply with the dark shadows beneath the trees.

I recounted my very first trip into this country. It
was in the high heat of midsummer. Every open glade was

ablaze with wild blue lupins and brilliant red Indian
paintbrush. The rock rabbits were on the rock slides
gathering their store of winter hay. The shining black
bears with their playful cubs were tearing up old dead
logs in search of ants. The beavers and their kits were
busy in their ponds, now filled with water weeds.

All these warm and glorious reflections enfolded
me in quiet contentment. Yes, I had been enriched a
hundred times over in this high country. I was so glad.

Smoothly, swiftly, silently the Sonata soared down
the almost-empty road. It astonished me to see so little
traffic. It seemed my Father had made special provision for
us to pass this way once more in utter peace and serene
quietness. What a special pleasure!

Soon we were down out of the main coastal range
running freely along the banks of the mighty Fraser River.
Here the fields were green, the first maples were breaking
out in bud, and the native wild currants were already
blushing pink and white with spring blossoms. Spring
fever swept through me, for I was back in familiar terrain.
Forty-five years ago I had lived in this valley, doing crop
research for the federal government at their experimental
research station across the river.

From there on, down to the sea edge, houses and
factories and shopping malls were taking over the land.
Traffic congestion increased. Highways and power lines
now spread a web of civilization and commerce across the
countryside where in my youth I hunted pheasants in
the fields and grouse in the woods. I remembered vividly
the cry of the geese coming in to feed on the green
meadows. And a great wave of sadness swept over me.
Yet I reassured myself that those had been glorious years
and that I was indeed a privileged person to relish this
great delta before "progress" brought so much change and
contamination.

At last we left the last of the civilization behind.
The road ran out on an embankment built into the sea.
The pungent aroma of seaweed in the sun, of ozone off

the windblown waves, swept into my nostrils. I was back by the sea again. The sea that had restored my strength so often. The sea that had sustained and nourished my soul. The sea that I loved with such a passion.

Thank You, Father, for bringing me back again. I was richer for it!

Poison Oak
and
Oatmeal

*E*XACTLY A WEEK AGO THIS MORNING, under a clear blue sky and with soaring spirits, I left for my first long spring excursion into the Northern Rockies. It was eight long months since I was last able to spend time high on the Continental Divide. So, as of old, I was charged with excitement, thrilled to be free again to ramble around on the roof of the earth . . . in company with deer, elk, mountain sheep, and bears.

It turned out the weather was perfect: settled, clear, calm, with a lovely sprinkling of new leaves and fresh flowers decorating the mountain valleys. The mountains themselves impressed me as being adorned in unusual breathtaking beauty. The heavy snows of the long, harsh winter still clung to their crests, which now glittered with brilliance against the intense blue sky.

I do not remember ever being so thrilled by my beloved mountains. Though I have been climbing, hiking, and roaming across these northern ranges for some 35 years, half my lifetime, they still stirred me to the depths this spring. What a fortunate, blessed, happy man I was!

How honored to be strong enough and fit enough to roam at will across the high country in my seventies! Perhaps the acute awareness of such a rare privilege heightened my delight.

Again and again there tumbled from my lips the profound gratitude I felt within. "Thank You, my Father, for such uplift, such joy, such utter delight in all You have created."

Everywhere I turned there was grandeur and glory: soaring ice fields untouched by man; hanging glaciers of intense blue; giant ice falls resembling mammoth cathedral organs; rushing streams adorned with banks of snow and ice.

Closer at hand herds of elk, deer, and wild sheep were moving up into the mountain meadows. Soon each elk cow, each deer doe, each mountain ewe would search out her own private spot to drop her newborn on the fresh green grass. Already the first buttercups, wild crocuses, and mountain anemones were bursting through the brown litter of last year's dead grass.

The buds on the pines, spruce, fir, and mountain hemlock were bursting from their brown sheaths in soft and tender green shoots. The air was redolent with their fragrance, and in the valleys the pungent perfume of poplars and balm of Gilead wafted softly on the spring air. The whole upland world was like a veritable paradise.

Then the unexpected happened!

Suddenly there was a serious problem in paradise.

On the third day out my whole body began to burn, except for my face and neck.

The scalding, flaming, itching irritation extended from my upper arms to the very soles of both feet. I stripped off my clothes in desperation. Standing unclad in a white drift of new snow, I looked like a man burned bright red by the sun. Great splotches of scarlet eruptions covered my arms, thighs, and feet. I was literally on fire with a massive dose of poison oak poisoning.

Where I had encountered it I did not know. Across the years I have suffered from this plant in various parts of the country. I have been so infected that my face and eyes were no longer recognizable, so swollen, distorted, and inflamed were they. But always before I was close to home and within early reach of help.

Not so today. I was high in the mountains, alone, and some 400 miles from home. At once I plunged into the soft snow. I rubbed it all over my body. It cooled and soothed my skin. Quickly I dressed.

Without delay I stumbled quickly through the rough wooded terrain and returned to my car parked off the road. If I was fortunate the infection would not spread to my face and eyes. It would be nip and tuck to try to get home alone. Already the day was late, with the sun settling over the western ranges. So part of the travel would be night driving. The Sonata would have to fly as swiftly as an eagle headed for its nest.

And she did, in magnificent power. Never had I driven a smoother, more responsive vehicle. She quite literally soared over the high passes, down the deep winding mountain valleys, headed for home.

At the very first phone I could find along the way I called Ursula to say I was hurrying home, four days ahead of time. She could expect me about 11:30 P.M., and please have a bath, laced heavily with baking soda, ready for me.

Precisely at 11:20 I pulled into our garage. My face and eyes were still clear. It had been a remarkable respite. Best of all, I was safely home. Cheri met me with her big smile . . . mingled with a deep look of concern.

During the night she had called several close friends asking them to pray for my safe travel home. One had told her that as a small child her aged grandma always boiled up oatmeal, put the hot porridge in a cheese-cloth container, then applied the liquid extract from the oats to her inflammation. We should try it.

I shed my bush clothes in no time flat and plunged into the bath, but found no relief. Meanwhile Cheri made up a huge bag of gelatinous oatmeal. Carefully I rubbed its slippery fluid over my inflamed body. It was a messy business. To make matters worse it quickly dried like glue.

My treated feet actually attached me firmly to the floor so I felt glued to the spot. No wonder my parents, in forcing me to eat oatmeal porridge as a small boy, always added the comment "It's good for you. It really sticks to your ribs!" They no doubt spoke more accurately than they realized.

At any rate, wonder of wonders, in a matter of just a few minutes the awful burning and itching began to subside. Within half an hour most of the pain was gone, and for the first time in all my horrible encounters with poison oak, I experienced absolute relief from its agony. It literally was a minor miracle for me.

Across the years I had tried every possible sort of antidote, with only marginal relief. In all that time not a single soul had ever mentioned oatmeal applications. It seemed strange indeed that such good news could be kept so secret for so long.

Perhaps, like the Gospel, God's Great Good News of His loving antidote for the awful poison of man's deep defilement, it is too simple, too homely, to believe. Most people in their despair will not even try it. As for me in my extremity, I was glad to try the oatmeal.

When I awoke the next day two things really astonished me. The first was that the largest eruptions had virtually disappeared overnight. Second, I looked just like a leper, with great blotches of dry, cracked skin scattered over my body. But the most wonderful sense of respite and restoration engulfed me.

With several more applications of oatmeal, plus taking large quantities of Vitamin C, I was completely well within three days. This was unheard-of before. Always it had taken a week to ten days to recover.

Simple, plain, old-fashioned oatmeal was the secret, along with simple, plain, old-fashioned prayer and faith in our Father!

The Letter

$\mathcal{L}$ETTERS OF EVERY SORT AND DESCRIPTION come to me from all over the world. Some are from friends or family. Others are written by total strangers who have read my books or listened to my tapes. Some are sent by those whom our Father has touched deeply in our times together.

Yesterday one of these latter joyful messages came in the mail. Our postbox is not at our house. It stands with a cluster of others, out on the shoulder of the main road, about a block from our home. One of the simple, rich delights of the day is to walk over there to fetch the mail. The views along our road, which hugs the hilltop, are bold, sweeping, and uplifting. Far below, the lake lies in its mountain basin like a polished mirror, reflecting the rugged mountain ranges around us. The rocky hills rise up around us on every side. And here, as I tramp over for the mail, meadowlarks sing from the hill and California quail call from the sagebrush.

I never know what sort of messages will come in

the mail. But yesterday brought a special letter, full of good news and great good cheer.

When I opened the envelope, out fell two sheets of brilliant yellow paper. Inscribed on them in bold, black ink were half-a-dozen paragraphs. The script was powerful, direct, and positive, belying the age of the writer as almost 85 years of age.

Ursula and I first met her and her sister when we began to attend a small community church in California. They came from sturdy British stock, bearing themselves with that regal dignity which is the hallmark of royal lineage. Both sisters had brilliant minds and keen intellects. They had long been considered two of the leading stalwarts in the little church.

But very soon I was sure the elder one did not know the living Person of the Living Christ. She had never encountered Him as the very light of her life.

Then one night, after leading an open-discussion Bible study, she came to me privately and whispered softly, "Phillip, please tell me, exactly what is a Christian?" Not only did I tell her then and there, but I took the time to write it all out in full, giving all the precise Scripture passages that conveyed God's message of love and forgiveness for us in Christ.

She took this matter very seriously. She had been a highly esteemed teacher, so she studied the material carefully. About a month later she met me at the chapel, her face aglow with a newfound assurance. In her abrupt, clear, direct way she declared, "Phillip, at long last in this long life of mine I finally know not only *who I am*, but far more important, *whose I am*. I now belong to Christ. I am His!" My spirit soared with thanks.

The years went by. We left California. Time and advancing years made their mark on her, yet still her spirit was quickened.

Then suddenly this past winter she entered a cancer clinic for chemotherapy. And this is part of what the bold black lines on the bright yellow pages had to say:

Phillip, I thought you would enjoy sharing with me in my recent experience.

The amazing change that has come about in me is that I sense that God, the all-powerful source of the universe, is present with me day and night. He is my source of energy, which will return back into my body, now almost 85 years old. His presence is warm and real. My sister feels the same way. We are working together to the end of our earthly journey.

He is our light! His peace within is the most glorious feeling that I have ever had. We accept what comes in the days ahead, knowing that The God we love and respect is with us and keeping us safely.

I wish I could share this with you in person. Thank you, Phillip, for being my mentor, who led me to This Great Light.

Love and respect,

Is it any wonder that this little letter made the whole day bright with supernatural light for me as well? Are we surprised that Christ Himself declared forcibly, "I AM THE LIGHT OF THE WORLD"? Here, now, in undeniable testimony and living truth those words have been validated, both for my friend and for me. Are people surprised when some of us say unashamedly that we revel in His Presence?

Country
Church,
Country
Preacher

*F*OR YEARS AND YEARS I HAD crossed the high mountain range lying to the west of our valley, and gone down into the villages below to hold Bible studies. At first we began the classes in private homes. But the numbers attending grew steadily until we were meeting weekly in the local community hall.

Those were precious interludes, joyous times when Christ moved among us and touched lives at great depths and in special ways. Often it was my secret longing that some young man would feel called of God to come to the remote little valley and establish a permanent work in this difficult, challenging community.

It had been notorious for its tough characters and rugged frontier families. Most of them were ranchers, loggers, miners, and farmers. It seemed that almost every attempt to start a church had floundered. The thought saddened me. From time to time I spoke to others about my concern and hope that our Father would call someone to help.

Then suddenly it happened. We had been away for years, but the first time we passed through the area I noticed a new country church built by the side of the road. My spirit soared in gratitude and joy. My Father had been faithful to honor the deep desires of my soul.

Last Sunday was our chance to visit this place of worship. As we drove through the mountains I clearly remembered the scores and scores of times we had driven this route through sleet and storms, through blinding blizzards and the grim darkness of winter nights. But today we were going through in the warm sunshine of April, with spring flowers and green grass on the slopes.

As we pulled into the churchyard I immediately recognized people who had come to our classes years before. They greeted us with warmth, smiles, and generous hugs. It was such a special inspiration to see so many young families crowding into the simple little structure. Children of all ages almost equaled in number the adults in the congregation.

What surprised me most was how well they all behaved during the cheerful service. There were no outcries, no whimpering, no fussing. It was as if all the youngsters thoroughly enjoyed the service. A gentle atmosphere of peace and contentment filled this humble country church.

Then the young pastor began to speak, drawing his sermons from copious handwritten pages. Almost at once the phrases he used and the truths he stated came back to me like echoes from the past. Almost sentence for sentence—in fact, word for word—he was simply reading whole passages from one of the books I had written 15 years before.

At first I did not know whether to be sad or to be glad. Sad because he relied so heavily on what some other man had been given by God, or glad to think that even in this little country chapel Christ's Word to me, printed so long ago, was bearing fruit still in this unlikely spot.

Not wishing to embarrass the dear young pastor,

we left quietly, without letting him know who we were. But one day soon I shall slip over the mountains to see him privately. He will be encouraged to ruminate quietly over God's Word for himself; to draw strength for His Master's service directly from His truth; to experience the thrill of being so refreshed in spirit himself that he in turn will be a blessing to His people.

We drove home in joyous contentment. We had been repaid in full for the time and effort spent here years ago!

Such are the wondrous ways of our Father.
His surprises come in such lovely encounters.
His bonuses of delight stir our souls.

No service ever rendered to Him in humility of heart or sincerity of spirit is forgotten. At some future time, in some special manner, He more than makes up for all that has been spent on His account and for His people.

Just as we were about to drive out of that little churchyard a tough, lean, sunburned rancher rushed over to me. He thrust out his hard hand in a hearty greeting, his face wreathed in smiles. "I remember clearly everything you ever taught us in your classes here years ago," he blurted out, a bit overexcited. "I especially remember the stories you told to illustrate God's spiritual truths." I could only grin and give hearty thanks.

Unknown to him, he had left me a richer man than when I came to worship in that simple place that morning. I will look at this little church with fond affection and a mellow mood for the rest of my days. Part of my life, long buried in that tough valley, had sprung up into new life under Christ's care. How dear He is!

Rain
in the
Desert

*O*UR RUGGED AND SOMEWHAT REMOTE MOUNTAIN country is a restricted region comprising one of the few areas of true desert in Canada. It extends only about 30 miles north of the United States border. Still, its sagebrush, greasewood, cactus, and desert rock roses are sure evidence that this is the northernmost extremity of the true Sonora Desert that reaches deep down as far south as Mexico.

Here annual precipitation, including all our winter snowfall, is actually less than 12 inches. Summer weather finds the thermometer above 100 degrees on the hottest days. Only the presence of our lovely lakes, our little mountain streams, and our forested hills provide respite from the heat and dryness. And, I should add, so do our occasional showers of rain, which pass through quickly, lingering only a few hours, before blowing over the ranges.

But rain here is precious. It is oh so refreshing! It is always, always welcome. All the world revels in its benefits ... especially if it falls persistently overnight to leave the earth glistening with moisture, redolent with the lovely fragrance of grey sage and ponderosa pines.

It rained all last night!

Not in a driving downpour, but with the gentle, soft, persistent patter of tiny raindrops washing the windows and soaking the soil.

This morning every blade of grass, every leaf on shrub or tree, every native or domestic flower, is turgid with moisture, glowing with life, beautiful to look upon. The rain has washed away every clinging particle of dust. It has quickened every living thing with new life and energy.

Rain in the desert always reminds me of the serene and lovely refreshment that comes to my life from Christ Himself.

In drought and in dryness He comes to me bringing the bounties of His own precious presence, to refresh and to restore.

In times of stress and distress, in days of weariness and waywardness, it is the refreshment of His presence, the renewal of His peace, that, like the rain, restore my soul. There are those hours when, like a tree stricken with heat and drought, I stand before Him, fully exposed, fully extended, open to receive again the gracious bounty of His grace. It is the still dews of His Spirit which must descend in refreshment upon my spirit, the gentle rain of His own abundant life which again must engulf and overflow my entire being.

With His coming there also comes cleansing; there comes replenishment of life within; there comes vigorous new growth in godliness.

He does not disappoint me. He comes that I might have His own abundant life. And this I have in knowing Him in quiet communion.

Rain in the desert!

Heavy Horse Country Fair

*T*HE ANNOUNCEMENT WAS AN OBSCURE LITTLE piece tucked away on the back page of the local paper. I spotted it by chance as I quickly perused the pages early in the morning (there had been no time to read the paper the day before). A heavy draft horse show was to be held that very day in a small ranching community about 60 miles across the mountains.

Quickly I made up my mind to go. I have always had an enduring love for the gentle giants that I learned to harness, care for, and drive as a young newcomer to Canada. I had gathered maple syrup in the spring snow of the northern Maple Bush County. I had plowed and harrowed and seeded the rugged rocky areas of a frontier farm with heavy horses. I had even endured a terrifying runaway with a wild western team while mowing. I had raked and hauled and stacked hundreds of tons of hay with draft horses. I had paid a good part of my way through university by tending a stable full of some of the finest brood mares ever bred on this continent. I retained an enduring affection for heavy horses.

But I did not want to go to the fair alone; this was a celebration to be shared.

It would be a festival for old fellows fond of Percherons, Clydesdales, Belgians, and whatever else.

Though it was early, I awakened an aged friend from his sleep. I offered to pick him up, along with a brown bag of sandwiches he should prepare, and we would be off on a lark. He was thrilled!

Under a spring sky we drove down our valley, then climbed into the high ranching country to the east. The rangeland was at its best, bursting into fresh and tender greens. All the while we exchanged boyhood yarns and told fond stories of our various escapades on farms and ranches 50 years ago.

The recollections, like precious gems kept in a vault, tumbled out of our memories into the brilliant, exciting light of the moment. We were experiencing renewal, rejuvenation, bright delight, potent pleasure. Such are the benefits of memories relived in sharp and scintillating retrospect. This was and this is one of those splendid and lovely bonuses which our Father bestows on His earth children. What unalloyed joy!

We laughed, we joked, we chuckled, we grinned from ear to ear. And without shame of any sort we also saw a tear or two of pure pleasure.

How many people in our world today could know, relish, and exult in the sensations that swept through our souls? How many could comprehend the sheer ecstasy of relived days when we challenged the frontier with our own brute strength and the straining muscles of our giant teams? Only a few—very few!

We knew this to be so when we pulled into the inviting fairgrounds and parked beneath the pines. The whole place was tidy and spotless. New-mown grass was emerald green, decorated by a sprinkling of brilliant golden dandelions. Meadowlarks sang in the trees. The river rumbled in its spring flood along the edge of the paddocks.

But only a handful of people were present, and already the judging was under way.

Giant geldings, stormy, snorting stallions, and great gentle mares were being paraded around the ring. Each had been groomed, trimmed, decorated, and adorned for this special day. The flashy halters and the brass-and-silver-studded harnesses sparkled in the morning sun.

A whole page of pageantry was lifted from the past.

We old-timers were transported back in time at least half a century.

Every hour of the day was relished.

It astonished both of us to see such magnificent horses in such a remote northern valley. Could it be that people, weary and jaded by the jazzy lifestyle of modern cities and the empty pretense of the jet set, were turning back to the land, to horses, to find peace and fulfillment?

Because there were comparatively few visitors it was possible to saunter gently through the stalls, admiring the magnificent horses close up, talking softly to their owners. Every person we spoke to came from a family farm or self-owned ranch. They loved their charges, they loved their life, they loved their land.

All of this put a special patina on the events of the day. We were not being entertained by a gaudy show put on to display the wealth and prominence of some multi-million-dollar breeders. We were being welcomed into the wondrous, warmhearted world of our frontier forebears.

Again we were reliving a humble chapter from the past. We relished the rattle of the farm implements used to break and tame this northern wilderness. We gloried again in the splendid strength and mighty muscles of horses that weighed nearly a ton apiece, but were gentle and responsive to the master's touch.

When we drove home in the late afternoon both of us were still in spirit, pensive in soul, mellow in mood.

It had been a day of pure delight.
We had shared our Father's bounty again.
Our lives were enriched beyond measure.

Little Book
from
Far Away

*T*HE LITTLE BOOK, BOUND IN A plain pink cover, fell out of the brown envelope into my hands. The words on the jacket were in strange syllables and peculiar phrases beyond my understanding. But at the bottom, in clear, unmistakable form stood my name.

Inside the little volume the paper was poor and easily torn, the print uneven, the workmanship crude— obviously a homemade production. But behind all of this lay a simple story of God's grace and compassion.

With the book came a lengthy letter from a Christian worker in Thailand. On one of his tours of duty into Vietnam he had carried in his case a copy of my book *A Shepherd Looks at Psalm 23*. During his travels God's gracious Spirit had spoken to this worker profoundly through the book. So in visiting with one of the Vietnamese pastors, who also spoke excellent English, he shared the contents of the book.

The man asked if he might borrow the volume

and read it for himself. The book was left with him and somewhat forgotten by the worker from Thailand. But evidently the Vietnamese pastor had far from forgotten the book. Instead, he was so deeply moved by its message that he had set to work and translated it into his own language in his own home.

More than that, at his own expense and with his own meager income he undertook to make up 1000 copies. Then he proceeded to pass them out to every Christian leader in the country that he came across. The little books were warmly received and joyously shared with others. In His wondrous ways our Father used the little books to uplift, encourage, and cheer His people in that war-torn land. All of this had been unknown to me.

In humility and joy I bowed my spirit in awe and wonder.

From day to day as I beseech Christ to use the books He has enabled me to write for His people, I often wonder just how those prayers are answered. Here was a case in point. Here was His gracious, gentle Spirit nudging a simple pastor in a far-off place to spread the great good news of our Father's love to those who so desperately needed to hear it. Here was the special wonder of His ways in our weary old world.

Some people might have been shocked to think anyone would be so bold as to plagiarize a whole book. I was not! I was thrilled that in this unusual manner, others far away were able to come to Christ and find in Him a great and loving Shepherd for their souls.

There is a very unusual sense of adventure in discovering how our Father accomplishes His work on earth. He uses the most unlikely people in some of the most unusual places to achieve most astonishing results.

My part, in quiet faith, is to trust Him for it.

He does not disappoint me.

Rather, He delights me with joyous surprises and happy adventures! How dear He is!

Wild Gardens

*O*UR RESIDENTIAL LOT IS QUITE LARGE, located high on a hill with a sweeping panorama all around us. The original owners had landscaped the street side with formal lawns and choice evergreens, both trees and shrubs. Fortunately for me, the steep side of the land was left untouched, untamed in its natural state.

Here a surprising variety of wildflowers, shrubs, and trees flourish on the wild, windswept slope. There are ponderosa pines, Olalla bushes, desert greasewood, rabbitbrush, and grey sage. Each perfumes the air with its own delicate fragrance. Among the native flowers there are gorgeous displays of rock roses, golden balsam root, wild pinks, and desert lilies.

These follow each other in quiet succession across the mountain seasons, lending beauty to our surroundings, all with virtually no special concern or care from me. Occasionally I will remove encroaching plants of wild mustard and Russian knapweed, which are introduced weeds. And to counteract their invasion I bring home pocketfuls of wild seeds from my hikes in the high

167

country to scatter at random over the bare spots. All of this has added to the profusion of our blooms.

One of my favorite escapades is to slip away softly for several hours and explore a mountain meadow or upthrust ridge still wild and still unspoiled. There are many such wilderness spots in our mountain terrain. Few of the local people seem to know about them, and even fewer seem to care to expend the energy required to hike into them. So they are special areas of gentle peace and wondrous serenity within close proximity to my home.

For me this is a rare delight in our crowded world. I feel honored and blessed to live in such a lovely region of the continent.

Yesterday was one of those special, enchanting interludes when the overwhelming urge swept over me to head for the hills and some of their wild gardens. Within 20 minutes I had parked in a secluded spot off a quiet ranch road and was climbing the lower slopes of some austere cliffs that daunted most visitors. But I knew the terrain well. Following an ancient deer track that climbed through the cliffs, I was soon over the summit and into virgin country seldom seen by man.

It was late May, and in our mountain realm the wildflowers are coming into their peak profusion. The past week had been damp and rainy, with squalls and showers blowing across the ranges. This upland world is a wonderland of skyscapes at such seasons. There is a tremendous sense of action, power, and dynamic energy in the cloud formations that dominate the sky.

Huge, wind-driven folds of high stratus clouds streamed northward from the southwest. Between their passing, brilliant sunlight dappled the hills, now verdant green beneath their scattered ponderosa pines. The valley I was in lay like a gorgeous, emerald-green garden bathed in sunlight with exquisite, clean, bracing, mountain air. I could see in every direction for at least 20 miles. Nowhere was there a single house in view, not a solitary human structure imposed on the landscape. It was native, pristine, mountain grandeur at its best.

In the far, far distance a solitary mountain range, higher than its fellows, sparkled white under last week's snow. But at my feet the range lay carpeted in a wild profusion of blue and white lupines, rock roses, blue gentians, wild cosmoses, and golden flowers of several species. I walked alone, bowed humbly in awe and wonder at so much natural splendor.

I came across one small outcrop of decomposing shale. To my amazement, by actual count some 121 sturdy, brilliant rock roses were flourishing in a space only 12 feet by 12 feet in extent. I could scarcely believe it. No man's hands had planted even one of them.

Later I climbed a ridge, where in a sheltered hollow between the granite parapets a whole garden of glorious lupines flourished in the sun. Not one had been bruised by a bull elk or stepped on by a wandering steer. They blew in the wind in wild perfection, unscarred, untouched by the hand of man.

I rambled on and found a perfect group of bright, brilliant rock daisies, pure gold, gleaming against a backdrop of shining peaks and green rangeland. It was a scene more exquisite than most mountain paintings. I wondered to myself if perhaps I was the only man who had ever paused to adore the scene.

As the hours passed with so much pure joy and unabashed delight in God's Wild Gardens, I began to reflect upon my own life. Perhaps I too was a bit like these wild gardens, not trimmed, not carefully tended, not precise, not exactly proper, but still wild, untamed, thriving in the freedom granted to me to grow under The Master Gardener's touch.

Perhaps some stray wanderer on the path of life had come across my rugged life and there seen a bit of our Father's wild beauty in an informal garden. I hoped earnestly, and prayed fervently, that I wore the royal robes of His righteous character with the same intense elan as the brilliant blue gentians beneath my mountain boots.

"O Father, allow me to be beautiful too, I pray, in my unusual, rough, and rugged way!

"Under Your care, even though still windblown and wild, may my life be winsome with Your love and mercy."

Gridlock
and
Gentle Shore

I HAD KNOWN THE LOVELY COASTAL TOWN for 45 years. When I came to visit there the first time as a young man it seemed I had stumbled into paradise. It was such a tranquil spot! Its homes were surrounded with peaceful streets shaded by stately trees. Each residence was set in a small jewel of a garden that bloomed with fragrant flowers most of the year.

Most of the people lived at a gentle pace, with their little boats to fish in the straits off-shore, their picturesque walks along the cliffs, and their great insular life mostly cut off from the crushing pressures of progress on the mainland.

But all of that had changed across the years. High-speed ferry service, frequent flights by commercial and private airplanes, and an influx of tourists and newcomers from all over the world had turned the town into a throbbing, pulsing, panting hive of human activity.

With the accelerated lifestyle came all the usual difficulties and tensions of modern metropolitan centers. Crime was on the increase. Police protection was no longer adequate. Drug dealing was becoming common. Prostitution flourished. Traffic congestion had reached impossible proportions. And the blight of pollution—on air, sea, and land—was everywhere apparent.

The full impact came home to me in explosive reality when I became trapped in an absolute traffic gridlock on a lovely spring afternoon. Not a vehicle could move. There were cars in front, cars behind, and cars on both sides, all running their motors in futile desperation but not one turning a wheel. It was a first terrifying traffic gridlock for me. And I knew then that the time for me to leave this lovely island had come.

It was astonishing to think that modern society could in ignorance, folly, and greed create such havoc in a place of peace. Yet I was also fully aware that what was happening here was in fact happening in hundreds of other communities across the country. The congestion and corruption spawned by our society and our much-vaunted civilization was ruining the earth. We were polluting our own nests and defiling our own habitat, in a world where my Father had provided so abundantly for our well-being.

Later that evening I found a brief interlude in which to slip down to the shore and seek out a quiet sheltered spot to think long thoughts. I picked a sun-warmed spot behind a great driftwood log, where I was sheltered from the wind. The sunlight sparkled off the waves, seagulls scavenged the shore, and the gentle ozone off the sea titillated my nostrils.

Such gentle times had restored my soul often across the long years of my sojourn in this spot. So once more the precious bounties of sunshine, solitude, sea air, and sharp seascapes worked their wonders in my mind, in my soul, yes even in my spirit. Surely our Father surrounds us with fresh new benefits each day if we will but open ourselves to receive His gracious gifts.

But I knew too, by deep, profound instinct, that this chapter of my life was coming to a close. The days beside the sea on this particular bit of beach were at an end. The place had become too packed with people, too crushed and convoluted by our civilization, too stained and polluted by "progress" to be pleasant any longer.

In a day or two I would depart for the last time, perhaps. Happily I had found another peaceful place to live, far off in the mountains. Up there was still ample room to climb the ranges and roam the forest.

In serenity of spirit I knew my Father had been kind to lead me there. I was at peace, content in soul.

Dreams

*A*LL OF US HAVE THEM!
At some stage in life our dreams are almost more real, more vivid, more compelling than life itself.

Not those weird nightmares and haunting thoughts that sometimes rouse us from sleep with strange sensations.

But rather, those vivid visions imparted in the stillness of our inner souls by the Spirit of God Himself . . . those long-range views of what we can become in company with Christ . . . those wide, thrilling, stimulating vistas of what can be achieved under our Father's care and by His strong hands.

My life has always been intertwined with dreams of this kind. Even from my early boyhood God gave me great expectations of what could be achieved under His inspiration. Of a surety I sensed and knew He had great purposes to accomplish with my life—not necessarily in sensational ways of startling proportions, but in quiet, gentle, gracious ways that would enrich others and satisfy my own soul with work well done for His honor and His pleasure.

A great part of the splendid adventure of my long and exciting sojourn upon the planet has been to see the dreams God gave me come to completion. In some cases I had to wait ten, twenty, or even more years to see them fulfilled.

But when they came to life and flowered into full and abundant fruitfulness I have been ecstatic with inner joy: that special and unique caliber of serene contentment in my Father's faithfulness to me as His son.

For in fact, in living reality His Word to me is vindicated in vital events of day-to-day life that impinge on my companionship with Him. The ancient prophet of old spoke utter truth nearly 3000 years ago when he declared on behalf of the Lord:

> I will pour out my Spirit upon all flesh; and
> your sons and your daughters shall prophesy,
> your old men shall dream dreams, your young
> men shall see visions.

> —Joel 2:28

God has poured out His Spirit in abundance upon my little life. He has quickened me, inspired me, given me the courage to prophesy (speak to others on His behalf). He has given me the wide visions of youth to see what His noble intentions were for me as a man. He has allowed me to dream dreams as an older person. Above all He has arranged for those dreams to come true in stirring ways and joyous delight.

Just three days ago one of those dreams leaped into life. A man who just recently gave his life completely to Christ came to share an evening with us. He and his wife had just returned from a special course in Christian discipleship they attended for three months in Hawaii. The classes had been held at a Christian center where men and women were prepared to go out and serve Christ all over the world.

Not only did he brim over with excitement, but he also brought with him his bulging notebook and a package of photographs of the campgrounds where they trained.

As my wife and I looked at the pictures and listened to his enthusiastic account, a profound upwelling of praise and gratitude welled up to my Father from within my spirit. Why? Why should I be so moved, so touched, so stirred?

Because 20 years ago, with the aid of two tough Filipinos, I had cleared that very site from the jungle. With straining muscles, sweat-stained clothing, and steel determination we spent our honeymoon toiling in that spot under blazing sun and torrential tropical rain.

I envisioned then the people who would come to that spot from all over the world to be grounded in God's Word.

I dreamed of the day when groups would assemble there to prepare for mission service all over the Pacific and far beyond. My part was simply to be the humble pioneer who would clear away the jungle growth and open the place to sun and wind and the purposes of my Father.

He did not disappoint me. He never does! He had made those dreams come to life. Now, 20 years later, every vision I had came true. In the twilight of my time, tears of pure joy tumbled down my cheeks. In unashamed gratitude and unabashed praise I lifted my voice to give hearty thanks for such ecstasy of soul.

Surely, *surely* His bounties come in lovely surprises and unexpected delight!

His name is honored and I am enriched!

These are the dreams of divine arrangement, dreams of divine design, dreams of divine indulgence that my Father fulfills for His child.

The
Phone Call

I HAVE A PROFOUND AVERSION TO TELEPHONES.

I never used a phone until I was 19 years old, and then only by force. Perhaps that is why they repel me. I grew up on a remote outpost in East Africa. We never had a telephone and managed very well without the clumsy black instrument.

I came to North America in 1939 to attend university and I had never held a phone in my hand. Yet most of my classmates seemed to spend hours on the phone, especially to their giddy girlfriends. It all seemed so strange and so absurd.

Then one day it happened. A huge fellow heard I had never used a phone. He decided the time had come to introduce me to this ugly, noisy invention. Grabbing me by the arm he dragged me into an old-fashioned phone booth, slammed the door shut, and held me hard inside. I was really terrified, as he threatened me not to move. He called up his sister, thrust the receiver in my hand, and ordered me to talk to her. I felt awkward and embarrassed speaking to someone I could not see. The experience left a residue of resentment that has taken years to erase.

I feel phones really are phony!

People can so easily pretend to be pleasant on a phone, when really they are otherwise. They can say one thing yet really mean another. They can so readily deny statements made under the guise of being misunderstood.

When using a telephone there is no visual eye contact. One cannot read the other person's facial expression. There is no chance to decipher his body language, which may well speak greater truth than his words do.

Phones are an insidious cover-up.

They enable people to pretend and deceive others.

They can exude charm even from the worst character.

Even more abhorrent is their intrusion into the peace and tranquility of our homes. The demanding jangle and persistent repetition of noise instantly command attention. Everything is suddenly dropped just to pick up the phone. So often the calls are little more than a petty request for information, a wrong number, or even worse, an outright invasion of one's privacy.

In our home there are certain segments of the day when we simply shut the world out completely. The phone is disconnected and we are assured peace and privacy for several hours at a stretch. I simply refuse to let this instrument of modern technology become a tyrant in our home.

Of course I am fully cognizant of all the so-called advantages offered by this invention. They have been of some value across the years. But I will not allow the phone to disturb a quiet evening by the fire, or a gentle visit with old friends, or even a quiet siesta after lunch.

Still, there are moments when a phone call can bring great good cheer. Yesterday afternoon was a case in point. I answered the machine and heard a longtime friend on the other end. He wanted to share a bit of good news with me.

His son was driving across the continent, heading for spring training camp nearly 2000 miles away from home. He was a strong, burly, big fellow who played on one of the major league football teams. To pass the time as he traveled in his powerful Camaro he had placed a tape in his deck from one of the Bible studies I lead in his community.

In the privacy of his high-powered car the gracious Spirit of the Most High overwhelmed him with a sense of Christ's presence. He broke down in awe and adoration. That night he phoned home to tell his folks.

They in turn called me. I was uplifted by that phone call!

Hearty
Laughter

*F*OR WEEKS, ALL SORTS OF PEOPLE had been in touch with us to see if they could come for a visit. It is that way in our part of the country. The warm sun of summer, the beautiful sky-blue lakes, the lovely clean sand beaches, the lush orchards with their abundant fruit, the rugged scenery of the mountain ranges—all attract visitors to the region, especially after the snow has melted and left its legacy of wildflowers.

But not all the would-be guests are individuals of sincerity and sensitivity. Often on the least little whim or slightest change of weather they will alter plans, call up casually, cancel arrangements, and offer some flimsy excuse not to come.

Twice this happened earlier this week. Even though we had made careful preparations to receive two couples, both called to say they would not be coming. Oh, that tiresome telephone, so often used to dodge and duck out of difficult decisions! How plausible people can seem on the phone. What play-acting and false pretenses they can participate in with impunity!

I felt especially sorry for Ursula. She had taken special pains to prepare well in advance for their arrival. She had a special menu in mind for each party. All the food had been procured. In fact she had even begun to make her exquisite coffee cake when the last call came. What now?

We wondered if we should invite several other local families to come over and share our special bounties. Then the phone rang again. It was a dear couple who lived down the hill just below us. They wanted to have a wee visit. Could we get together that evening? Of course we could—with joy and good cheer! So just at sunset they climbed the trail to our home and came in, all smiles.

For reasons not entirely clear to me, it seemed that all four of us were in a rather hilarious frame of mind. Perhaps simply because firm friends love to be together. Perhaps because recently this dear fellow had overcome a serious heart condition and was again gaining new strength under our Father's care. Perhaps it was simply because it was much more fun to be with rough-and-ready people who had pioneered in the far north, finding joy in the simple delights of life, than with polished professional people.

For over 30 years they had served the Indian tribes in the northern territories. They knew all about hardships, tough times, generous service, and good old-fashioned goodwill. They also knew how to laugh in adversity and chuckle in the face of misfortune.

Anyway, as we sat down to relish the fine fare that Ursula had prepared with so much care, we began to chuckle with irrepressible glee. It was as if we were four lighthearted youngsters caught up together in a joyous escapade. We laughed, we joked, we found endless fun in everything said until our sides ached and tears of unabashed happiness tumbled down our flushed cheeks. So much pent-up good cheer flowed from within that the entire evening was one of pure ecstasy.

Our friends stayed late. And when the hour came for them to leave, the golden moon hung low above the western ranges. They were determined to walk home in its gentle glow after all of us had exchanged warm hugs.

As we turned in for the night, I remarked to Ursula, "Darling, our Father knew how much we needed such hearty laughter!" For it was He who sent us such contented company. How much more fun to be with such friends rather than the starchy, stiff visitors who otherwise would have come.

Yes, yes, it was true: "A merry heart doeth good like a medicine!" And we felt as fit as two fiddles.

The
Dentist

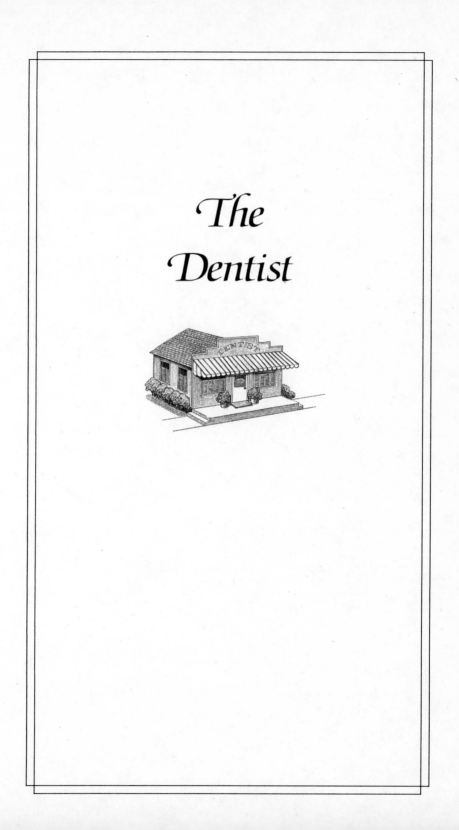

*W*HERE I GREW UP AS A lad, in the bush country of East Africa, there were no professional dentists. In fact, Dad, with a pair of rough forceps, removed hundreds of rotten teeth from the brave Africans who came to him for relief from their pain. They were sturdy characters who scarcely winced when he withdrew the offending teeth from their sturdy sockets. There were no niceties to modify the painful procedure: no needles, no novocaine, no freezing—only the grit and courage to hang on while the agonizing extraction took place.

That, too, was how my teeth were treated.
I was less stoic than my native friends.
So I howled and screamed in anguish.
At times it seemed my whole jaw was being
    torn apart.

Nor was this just imagination. For, unfortunately, the roots of my teeth were curved and locked fast in the bone of my jaw. So any extraction was sheer torture!

197

Even later in my life, when a professional dentist garbed in white and surrounded by shining instruments tried to pull a major molar, he was thwarted. Sweat poured from his brow as he struggled with the tooth. It would not yield, and finally it broke off, leaving the roots imbedded in my jaw. A few minutes later as I went to leave his office I suddenly collapsed in a heap on the floor. I came to with water poured over my head, my burning cheeks pressed hard against the cool cement floor.

So one can see why going to the dentist has never been a favorite pastime of mine. To circumvent such encounters I have tried to care for my teeth with special care and the most wholesome foods. To a large degree this has been successful, for I am now well into my seventies and still do not wear a plate.

Still, this past weekend a huge lower tooth went wild. Where would I turn for help?

For more than six years I had not had any dental work done, and I was hoping to get away with this pattern until the day I died. But it was not to be.

So quietly I entreated my Father to direct me to a dentist who, in the twilight of my life, could and would treat me with care, skill, and a minimum of pain. I had endured enough suffering from stubborn teeth.

At dawn I felt constrained to call a friend, a widow of a dear, dear fellow I had led to Christ years ago. Shortly before his death he had remarked to me that a dentist by the name of Dr. Jones had done superb work for him. The simple name "Jones" stuck in my memory. Would he possibly still be alive or even practicing in this high mountain valley? She assured me he was, down in a little village not far away. I arranged to come to her home later in the day to discuss just what procedures the dentist had used with her husband.

We were seated quietly in her living room, over-looking a lovely mountain lake, when the phone rang. Who should it be but Dr. Jones himself on the line? It was like a miniature miracle. Quickly she told him of my being there to ask about him, and could he possibly see me. His immediate response was "Send him over right now!" I liked that! Let's get at it and get it over with as soon as possible.

Our hostess, dear soul, had set out a lovely tea for us, ready to be served. All of it was forgotten in this sudden turn of events. Quietly we bowed our heads, held hands, and gave gentle thanks for such a beautiful provision of help in the hour of need. For we had found out that this dear dentist was not only an expert in his field, but also a devoted, loving follower of Christ.

In a matter of minutes Ursula and I were parked in front of the cute little yellow bungalow that housed his office.

The moment we entered, a sense of repose, quietness, and peace pervaded the place. For the first time in my life no apprehension gripped me like a vise. I felt at ease. The receptionist with shining face remarked softly, "We have been expecting you"—all of this without any sort of appointment. How graciously my Father had prepared the way for me!

A few moments later I met the doctor. I was drawn to him at once. His open countenance, his quiet smile, and his firm handshake assured me I had met a friend. "I have read many of your books," he remarked softly. "It is an honor to serve you!"

After scanning my teeth with meticulous care he looked at me tenderly and said, "If you will just put yourself in my care, I believe we can save all your teeth and preserve your health for many more years to serve God and His people." It seemed too good to be true. I was sure my stubborn teeth would have to be pulled out in pain to be replaced with a false set. What good news that dear dentist gave me!

His procedures were carried out with such precision that immediately I was set at ease. He had such a gentle rapport with his assistant. And between all three of us there flowed a palpable stream of joyous goodwill.

As the nurse prepared me to take several X-rays she remarked softly, "God works in mysterious ways His own wonders to perform in our lives!" And surely that was an obvious truth on this day in a dentist's office.

She slipped a recording of a magnificent classical piece into her machine. The soft melodies filled the room and enveloped my whole being in quiet repose. For the first time in my life I was at rest in a dentist's chair.

Perhaps this seems a small thing to most moderns, but for me as a wild son of the African bush, with all of its brutal blood and gore and suffering, this was pure peace from above. I knew I was among friends who cared!

First
Summer
Swim

*T*HOUGH OUR HOME IS SITUATED IN a northern mountain range, laced with lovely lakes, and nurtured by snow-fed streams, the summers are hot, hot, hot! Summer temperatures soar into the nineties, and on occasion exceed 100 degrees. Native cactus, sagebrush, greasewood, and even rattlesnakes thrive in the heat, but I do not! My body metabolism seems unable to adjust to the extreme heat. Like the marmots in our area, my only defense is to enter a state of semi-aestivation in which part of the summer is slept away in partial coolness down below the blazing temperatures above.

It also helps enormously to cool down my whole body by immersing it in clear, cool water. In this the lake nearby is an unparalleled pleasure. I have found a tiny hidden cove, with a stretch of sandy beach, where I slip into the cooling waters and find complete composure from the heat stress.

Part of the year this lovely lake is locked in ice. So it takes most of spring to warm up enough to swim in comfortably. This week, after a cool, cloudy, rainy June,

the lake was ready and so was I. The first day I went
down it dismayed me to see the surface yellow with a
heavy dusting of pollen from the ponderosa pines and
wild desert flowers. But several strong winds soon cleared
the waters. Then yesterday I slipped into the shining
depths and knew glorious relief again.

It was the first of many cooling interludes that will
extend well into fall, when the sumac blazes red amid the
rocks and the poplars glow with gold along the shore.

In the waters of the lake there is release and rest—a
gentle, gracious gift from my Father. How grateful I am
for this precious benefit, bestowed with such tender care!

Fieldstones

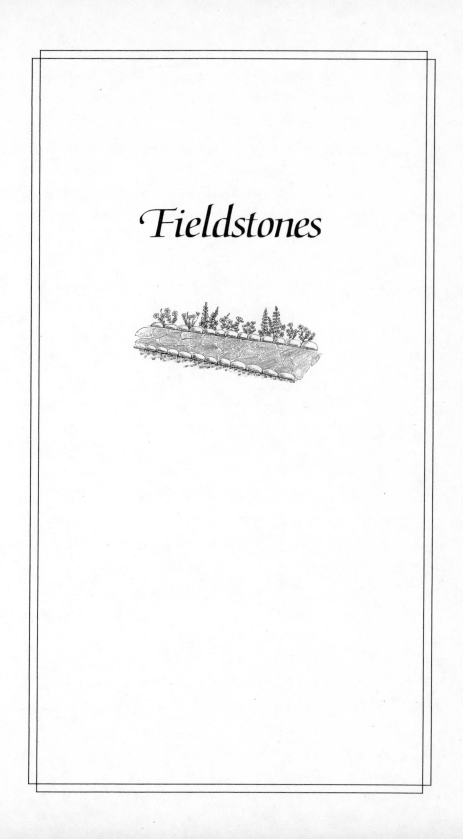

*O*UR REGION OF THE NORTHERN MOUNTAINS was once buried completely under a massive mantle of deep ice and enduring snow. As the ice age withdrew, so did the giant glaciers and massive snowfields. Behind them were left the great valleys of the mountain realm, with here and there gigantic moraines composed of sand, soil, and ice-ground rocks.

The soils so formed are rich in minerals from the earth's mantle. They account for the magnificent fields of alfalfa, the abundant orchards, and the rich gardens that adorn the district. But for every field, every flower bed, and every vegetable patch there are countless hours of labor, sweat, and cost to clear away tons and tons of fieldstones.

Most of this rock has found its way into building beautiful terraces, lovely retaining walls, and other fine decorative work such as handsome fireplaces or ornate garden paths. My summer project was to put a new path around the back of the house. It would be bordered with fieldstones and paved with the handsome red native shale that decomposed off the local rock cliffs.

But the fieldstones are no longer as plentiful and common as they once were; too many people have put them to good use. I needed just one more load to finish up my project. Where would I go? Where could the shining stones be found without undue difficulty?

Quietly I lifted my spirit in supplication for clear guidance. The clear impression came that I would find all I needed at the foot of the hill just below our home.

In complete confidence I slipped on a pair of tough leather gloves, climbed in the car, and drove down the steep road. In less than a mile I spotted a whole pile of rocks the exact size I needed just beside a neighbor's garden.

To my unbounded delight both he and his wife were out in the yard as I drove up. Without delay I came to the point. "Would you care to get rid of your rocks?" Their response was immediate. "Would we ever! We hand-dug every one of them out of the garden patch before we could even plant it!"

For a few moments we exchanged jokes and enjoyed some hearty chuckles about charging me a dollar for each large stone, while the smaller ones came at 50 cents apiece. And, of course, the whole transaction would have to be covered by a proper contract drawn up in a lawyer's office. What fun!

Amid the gales of laughter and goodwill I loaded up the trunk of the car until I felt the springs were at full capacity. Then, with a hearty handshake and glad goodbye, I was off up the hill.

Stone by stone I carried the precious prizes around the house and set them in place. The sweatdrops poured from my face and fell on the stones, but the job was being done. To my utter amazement and overflowing delight I had exactly enough in one load to finish the job. In fact only two small stones remained over to fill small chinks in another wall.

A small thing with common fieldstones.
No, a precious provision from my Father's
hand!
Through a clear inner compulsion, and
the gentle cooperation of kind
neighbors, the task
was taken care of in joy and
pleasure.

It is this sort of daily adventure that puts a keen edge on the events of daily living in company with Christ. He actually shares my life and I share His, even in something as simple as finding fieldstones for a garden path.

Never, ever, will I walk along that path without being reminded of His care. And, as I do, a warm smile of fond remembrance will lighten up my face.

Twenty-First Anniversary

*W*HEN CHERI AND I FIRST MET, it was as if two
waifs from faraway countries had come together
in the kindly, providential purposes of God. First of all,
both of us had traveled thousands of miles from our native
birthplaces to try to establish ourselves in the rather
rugged region of Canada's West Coast. She came from the
northern state of Eastern Germany bordering on the
Baltic Sea. I came from the sunburned plains and bush
country of Kenya.

· Neither one of us had a close-knit family to turn to
for support or encouragement. Cheri had been brought up
in a Christian orphanage as a solitary child from a family
most of whose members died from tuberculosis. She had
neither brothers nor sisters that lived. I was somewhat the
same in that my childhood memories were of austere
boarding schools with little else but drab dormitories and
stern discipline. Nor did I have brothers or sisters that
lived.

Our parents had passed on, so that in essence it
seemed rather special to have found each other. Added to

all of this was the formidable fact that both of us had
suffered very serious illnesses of life-threatening severity.
She had undergone prolonged treatment for cancer. I had
been afflicted with a variety of illness that had threatened
to terminate my life at a rather early age.

So when we married it was in the calm and sober
knowledge that our time together might well be very
short. In fact we sometimes felt sure that only a couple
of years remained for us to relish life. Because of this
we cherished our time and decided to celebrate on the
seventh day of each month. This is because we had
carefully chosen to be wed at 7:00 P.M. on the seventh day
of July, the seventh month, in 1970 (seven representing a
time of completion and fulfillment in God's economy).

Never in those distant days did either of us dream
we would be spared to serve Christ for more than 20
years. And just last week we celebrated a very special
milestones, our twenty-first anniversary (three times
seven).

We had hoped that somehow, in some unusual
way, it would be possible for us to slip away to a quiet
retreat for this lovely occasion. To our delight and happy
surprise, a letter came in the mail from a secluded lodge
high in the mountains. In it there was a voucher providing
us with three nights of free accommodation. The manner
in which they obtained our names remains a mystery,
which only adds to the deep delight of our celebration.

The day we drove over the mountains was perfect.
Cheri in her loving, caring way had packed a fine lunch of
hearty sandwiches. These we relished as we paused for
brief breaks beside the lakes and along the rivers on our
way. The mountains were still striped with snow at their
summits, and all the landscape was lovely after the late
spring rains.

That evening we dined in style in the giant dining
room with great windows overlooking the roaring river
below. To Cheri's ecstatic delight the Hawaiian wedding
song was played during our meal. Whether this was by

accident or design did not matter, for it was in Hawaii we had been married 21 years before. She looked radiant and serene sitting across the table from me. It seemed she was even more lovely than when we were wed. Such are the joys and special pleasures that Christ shares with those of us who follow Him.

Another evening we spent soaking ourselves like a couple of contented seals in a nearby mountain hot spring. Of old the Indians had come here to find relief from their ailments. Now we too bathed in the hot mineral waters and found ourselves refreshed and relaxed by the healing stream.

Then the day came to turn toward home. Most of the way we would be driving south, facing full into the fierce midsummer sun. It could become a tough trip over hundreds of mountain miles. So before retiring we besought our Father, if it so pleased Him, to send some clouds to shelter us from the burning heat.

To my special consolation I awoke to see trickles of rainwater running off the roof of the lodge. For roughly half the trip home we had cool, cool showers and heavy overcast that made driving a pleasure. But even more wonderful was the wildlife along the way that fed out in the open glades, not needing to shelter from sun and insects of a hot day.

Two magnificent bull elk especially surprised me. Here they were down in a valley marsh, when generally this time of year they are up on the alpine meadows. We saw deer here and there, and even a huge turkey gobbler strutting his stuff at the edge of the road in a remote forest area. Cheri suggested that we stop and pick him up for Thanksgiving. I assured her wild turkeys were not that easy to catch nor that tender to eat!

Smoothly, swiftly the Sonata swept us home. We stopped at a secluded roadside stand to pick up a basket of sweet Bing cherries. Their sweetness exploded between our lips, reminding us again of the great bounties which are ours in this remote mountain region.

Contented in mind and serene in spirit we pulled into our home on the hill. It had been such a cheerful interlude, rich in goodwill, replete with wonderful warm memories.

Such are the gentle, gracious gestures which our Father has poured out upon our simple life as His children. In quietness and contentment we relish each other's companionship, for we are more than man and wife: We are also brother and sister, father and mother, friend and companion to each other.

Apricots

IN ALL OF CANADA, WITH ITS predominantly cool climate, there are only two restricted ares where soft-stone fruits such as peaches, nectarines, and apricots flourish. One is the Niagara Peninsula of Ontario and the other is our warm Okanagan Valley of British Columbia. Our deep, rich, well-drained soils and hot summer temperatures produce bountiful crops of exquisite peaches and apricots.

Not until I was a young crop inspector, well into my mid-twenties, had I ever tasted a luscious, tree-ripened apricot. When I did, I became an instant devotee of this noble fruit. Few people have ever tasted the exquisite delicacy of an apricot bursting with its own sun-ripened sugars. Even fewer have known the pure pleasure of picking this delectable fruit from a tree whose branches hang heavy with the golden harvest.

I say this in sincerity because apricots are such a soft, perishable crop, with most of the fruit picked commerially when it is only about 20 to 30 percent ripe. The apricots are still quite green and the sugars are not yet fully formed, so the store-bought product is rather dry, flavorless, and unpalatable.

Where we live, on the mountain edge of the high desert, apricots flourish. The trees, unlike many other soft-fruit trees, live to great antiquity. They are very tough, very hardy, able to withstand severe drought in summer and deep freeze in winter. I have found old, gnarled, veteran apricot trees that survived nearly a century on a remote homestead in the hills. This they have done without being watered or cared for by any man. Year after year their fruit fed the crows and bears.

Apricots ripen during the hottest weeks of the year. Something of the intense golden sunlight is reflected not only in their gorgeous apricot colors but also in their sweetness.

And every summer the search is on to find a tree or two where they have ripened to tantalizing perfection. Apricots are not nearly as common as apples, pears, peaches, or plums, so it is not always easy to find the fruit near at hand.

But we have been blessed with gracious neighbors who shared their bounty with us. Last summer was a bumper year. Cheri and I picked buckets and buckets of the gorgeous red-gold fruit for fresh eating and preserves. For years I have felt that Ursula's home-made apricot jam was the finest in the world, an absolute treat to one's taste buds.

Last winter was very severe. Extremely high winds, low temperatures, and other adverse weather had damaged the fruit buds on the trees. The prospects of any crop at all this summer were poor. In fact most growers claimed there would be no apricots. I had more or less accepted this idea and adjusted myself to the thought that we would have to do without. Imagine summer without this superb fruit!

But then just a few days ago a dear fellow called up to say he had some apricots for us. I was ecstatic! But even more than that, in his wanderings he had come across some steep vacant land where three apricot trees, not touched at all, were laden with fruit.

Two evenings ago, just at sunset, I went down to pick the fruit pail full. The crop astonished me! The branches bowed down almost to the ground, loaded with golden fruit. The apricots were of superb flavor, fully ripe, ready to fall into my eager hands.

A tremendous, intense sense of gratitude and thanks enfolded my spirit. Again we had apricots in abundance. What a glorious gift not only from our friend who truly cared, but also from our Father, who nourishes us with such splendid fruit, free for the picking.

Again summer is complete. And I grin with pure pleasure every time I savor the golden flesh of my favorite fruit!

Summer Storm

$\mathcal{A}$S July moves slowly into August, the summer heat intensifies in our valley. All the surrounding hills, tinted with green by the spring rains of April, May, and June, turn a severe brown as though seared with the burning sun. Rocks, bare soil, and shadeless slopes absorb the heat of summer, radiating it back into the atmosphere until the whole earth pants with thirst.

Slowly, surely, and steadily the temperatures
rise.
Foliage flags and wilts and dries.
Birds, mammals, and man seek the shade.
All of us wait and hope and long for
rain.

Sometimes the first hint that a storm is on its way is an oppressive, intense stillness in the air. Not a leaf stirs, but hangs heavy and limp under stress. Not a bird note rises in the heat waves shimmering above the land.

Then suddenly there comes a fierce hot wind from the southern desert wastes. It picks up tumbleweed, dry mustard plants, and even drier dust, flinging them at random across the brown and barren hills.

Ominous clouds begin to gather above the higher ground. Brilliant, wide, spreading sheets of lightning explode over the landscape. Thunder rumbles and tumbles along the ridges and rolls like a battle drum down into the valleys. Stark stabs of electrical energy zigzag across the darkening sky. The entire atmosphere crackles and explodes with the startling ignition. Suddenly the whole world is alight with celestial fire.

Two nights ago Ursula and I stood at the windows, gripped by the glory and grandeur of such a divine display. The entire valley sweeping north and south for roughly 50 miles was illuminated with intense white light almost as bright as the midday sun. "This must be what it will be like when Christ returns in power and splendor," we whispered to each other.

"Yes, yes!" The thought swept through my spirit like a sheet of lightning itself. "How desperately, how urgently our dusty, drab, dreary old world needs a summer storm of spiritual illumination to sweep across it. The darkness deepens, the despair degrades mankind, and we stand stressed by the sin and sordidness of our society. Come quickly, oh Christ! Come in power! Come in mercy and majesty to restore Your honor upon the planet! Come in grace and forgiveness to refresh us again."

Hour upon hour the electrical storm swept over us. It surrounded us in enfolding energy. Plumes of smoke began to rise above the ranges across the lake. Forest fires, grass fires, and brushfires were being ignited by the lightning strikes that shattered trees, splintered rocks, and set the world on fire.

But then there came another sound . . . a sweet sound . . . a reassuring sound. Raindrops on the roof. Raindrops on the trees outside our windowpanes. Raindrops on the wind—splattering, shattering, streaming down the glass in silver rivulets.

First the stillness.
Then the wind.
Next the fire.
Now the refreshing
rain.

This is always our Father's sublime order. But most of us want to short-circuit the current of His presence and His power. We want the easy way, the cozy, comfortable way.

Hour after hour rain poured from the sky. At times every cloudburst was lit up to view like a giant display on a celestial screen. It took one's breath away in awe and wonder.

At dawn the whole earth pulsed with new life. Every tree, shrub, and blade of grass sparkled clean and cool and shining in the sun. The nitrogen-rich downpour had rejuvenated the whole world. Coyotes sang in the hills. Birds sang on the wing. And I sang in my soul with pure joy and upspringing gratitude.

Surprise
Parcel

*T*HE PHONE JANGLED INSISTENTLY, ALMOST AS a command. Deep in study, downstairs in my office, I was reluctant to drop everything and go up the spiral stairs to answer it. But the demanding sound persisted. So I assumed that the call was important enough to make me drop my work.

Galvanized into action I raced up the stairs, hurtled across the house, and lifted the receiver with gasping breath. The caller was unknown to me. I was sure he had the wrong number and told him so. But like the persistent jangle of the phone, he insisted he had the right party. What was more, he informed me a special courier had just dropped off a parcel for me at his store in the nearby village. Would I please pick it up?

Since I was not expecting any parcel I was a little mystified. What was even more puzzling, the name of the sender was unknown to me. And even more intriguing, why did the courier not deliver it to my door, instead of to a store in the village?

In an act of feeble faith I agreed to drive in and pick it up, feeling at the same time there must be a mistake somewhere. It all seemed so absurd!

When the parcel was handed to me I noticed it came from a publishing house far away. My spirits sank, and I thought to myself, "Just another manuscript from some strange editor who feels I should read it to write an endorsement!"

This happens quite often, and it seems odd to me. Why should anyone think my word is going to add weight to his work? It has always been my conviction that an author's work must stand or fall on its own inherent merit . . . not on what others say about it.

Without opening the package I tossed it on the back seat of the car. And, I was sure, it would be taken home to be tossed into the trash can.

Rather reluctantly I carried the parcel into the house, flung it onto the floor by the door, and went back to work. Like a crumb lodged in my craw, it irked me a bit the way any number of far-off editors felt they had the privilege to drop manuscripts on my desk in order to promote their own people. This had happened often across the years, and not once had one of them even so much as offered to pay a cent of reimbursement for the time and effort they expected to receive.

It was an odd notion—maybe one of those queer quirks taught by some half-baked professor of journalism in a two-bit writing course.

Still I decided the parcel should be opened. So, after lunch I took a sharp knife and slit open the sturdy wrapping paper. Out tumbled ten beautiful, glittering, gold-lettered paperback books. Nor were they from some unknown author in some faraway place. They were the latest edition of one of my own books. I could scarcely believe what I saw. What a surprise!

What startled me the most was their sudden arrival . . . so utterly unexpected, from so far away.

Up in the mountains where we live any delivery service is slow-slow-slow. Mail is notorious for taking endless time to reach us; parcels seem to come by Pony Express. Yet here in my hands I held ten golden copies of lovely design that had crossed the Atlantic, crossed all of Canada, and tumbled unannounced into our tiny village.

I was ecstatic with excitement. I could hardly wait for Cheri to come home and share the moment with her. It was one of her favorite books, and she too would be thrilled to see it done up with such sterling quality . . . a piece of work to honor our Father.

Here in our hands were ten more gift books to pass on to others who needed encouragement to truly trust Christ. These would not end up in the trash can. *Not everything is as it may appear!*

Somewhat astonished by what I saw spread out on the table before me, a sense of genuine remorse swept through my spirit. I had been too quick to come to a wrong conclusion about the contents of the parcel. I had been too hasty to attribute wrong motives to the sender. I had been too harsh in thinking wrong thoughts about far-off editors in faraway offices.

A deep inner constraint by God's gracious Spirit made me acutely aware that "Things are not always as they may appear." In contrition of soul I sought quiet forgiveness for my faults. In humility of spirit I quietly confessed my critical attitude. How wrong, wróng, wrong I had been!

With trembling fingers I ran my hands over the handsome books. Never, ever, in more than 40 years of writing, and the publication of more than 40 books, had I been so pleased with any pocket book bearing my name.

Obviously the publisher, the editor, and the art designer had given unusual care to the choice of cover for this work. Every element of the design had been developed with loving care and the highest quality of craftsmanship. The entire work bore the stamp of superb beauty and attractiveness.

Yes, some editor in some far-off place, unknown to me, had poured time and thought and loving attention into this project. It had been done not just for The Master's sake, but for mine as well . . . even though we had never met.

In that awareness I was humbled.

Our Father calls us to care, not only for those we actually meet and see and know, but also for those we never meet or see or know.

In the future my response to unknown, demanding editors in faraway places will be more cordial. Some of them must be saints . . . perhaps angels in disguise . . . perhaps. . . .

Glacial
Gravel

*F*ROM THE FIRST HOUR I WAS in this house I dreamed of adding a handsome patio to it. The house stood strong and secure on the crest of the rock ridge overlooking the lake. But it was a bit bare-boned, like an old-time Spanish villa, hunkered down on the hill defying summer sun and wrenching winter winds.

What it needed was a private patio, built of native stone, with a sheltering wall to break the force of the blustery breezes, and with some shade from the scorching sun. Here a man could come to relax quietly in almost any weather, and also find sweet solitude with long views across the shining waters to the rocky hills beyond.

Bit by bit the rocks were gathered, the wall was built with the help of a skilled stonemason, and a fine stone path was put in place around it. But what about the patio itself? How would it be finished for use? What material would provide the most practical floor?

All sorts of suggestions were offered by well-meaning friends. Put down tile. Lay cement. Cover it with indoor-outdoor carpet. Build a wooden floor. On and on the ideas

flowed. But none of them seemed to suit the purposes
I had in mind for this special spot. I wanted a place
that required minimum care yet provided maximum
enjoyment. It was a spot open to the sky, to rain, to sun,
that needed no painting, no sweeping, no special labor to
keep it looking natural and inviting.

For weeks the patio turned over and over in my
mind. It had been a sort of one-man project, so it was up
to me to finish it off in some simple yet suitable way. Odd
as it sounds, I had done everything except consult my
Master about the matter. When I did the solution came in
a flash: "Put in a floor of shining glacial gravel."

The thought thrilled me!
So uncomplicated!
Very practical!
Beautiful!

I set off in search of glacial gravel. I pictured a slide
somewhere in the hills where the shining material came
tumbling down the toe of an ancient glacial moraine.
Again I quietly petitioned my Father to guide me gently in
my quest. He did, for within three miles of my patio I
stumbled across exactly the gravel I wanted. It had lain
there for years, washed clean and lovely by a hundred
storms.

Every bit of it had to be shoveled by hand and
carried by hand out of the slide and down to my car. But
it would be worth every ounce of energy and every drop
of sweat demanded by such heavy labor. Anything truly
beautiful always costs an effort. So I was exhilarated with
the job and took careful pains to pick out the very finest
material.

Now and then I paused in my labor to look closely
at the water-smoothed stones, polished by the moving ice
ten thousand years ago. They glowed with a translucent
beauty comprised out of a hundred kinds of rock. They
had lain there untouched, unnoticed, unused for centuries.
Then one day a stranger came to pick them up with
special care to place them in his patio.

The gleaming, multihued gravel provided the perfect finishing touch to the patio. The raindrops would wash through these lovely stones and keep them sparkling. The sun would warm them swiftly so I could stretch out easily on their surface. And there would be no painting, no polishing, no sweeping—just plain, old-fashioned pleasure!

A thought, brief but arresting, swept through my spirit. Could it be that I too had been a bit of tough glacial gravel that Christ had picked up one day to lay down in the patio of His home? I hoped ardently that I brought Him as much pure pleasure!

Kingbird

*W*HERE WE LIVE BIRDS ABOUND. FROM early morning to late at night our upland world is enlivened not only with the songs of birds but also their flight all around our home. As I pen this paragraph a huge flock of wild geese gabble wildly as they glide down to the lake edge in joyous excitement.

We are located on the crest of a high rock ridge overlooking the lake. Powerful thermal updrafts build against the hill and all sorts of birds ride the wind right past our great windows. Several days ago an osprey swept past my office outlook, not more than 50 feet from my desk, clutching a fine trout in his talons, to feed his fledglings on the hill.

Bald eagles, golden eagles, ravens, crows, hawks, woodpeckers, blue jays, and numberless smaller birds all share our environment. They perch on our roof, sit on the balconies, and sweep across the lawns in pursuit of insects and nest in the trees and shrubs around us.

Of these, one of the most noticeable species has been a pair of kingbirds. Their sharp staccato cries, their aggressive behavior toward other birds, and their remarkable aerial acrobatics as they pluck insects out of the air are unique. They are not always the most attractive birds, but still we relish their company.

Then yesterday as we sat in the living room there was a sudden crash against the glass. A kingbird in full flight had flown into the window with high impact. It dropped to the deck below, a flightless bundle of bone, blood, and rumpled feathers.

Cheri and I raced down the stairs to retrieve the fallen warrior. It panted plaintively in great pain. We dropped cool water down its throat. But it was no use. The little aerial gladiator arched its back and died in my warm hands.

Tenderly, quietly, with genuine remorse I gazed at the still form, still warm, lying in my open palm. Never again would this remarkable little bundle of blood and bone and tissue clad in brilliant feathers hurtle through the air. Never again would it speed in sure flight across the mountains, deserts, forests, and fields to find its wintering ground in the far south. Never again would its defiant cry from the tip of the tall pine declare that spring was here, and that the kingbird had come back to claim his kingdom.

Gently I dug a small grave in the soft soil just below the spot where he often sat and sang. From the earth he had come; to the earth he now returned. This was the simple, inevitable cycle of birth, life, death.

■ ■ ■

Within a few hours of this intimate interlude, the earth-trembling news swept over the world that another kingbird had fallen. Gorbachev, defiant innovator of democracy in Russia, had been deposed in full flight. He was under house arrest, his future as tremulous as the tiny kingbird lying in my hands.

Only three days before one of our largest national newspapers, in a leading editorial, declared that *Pravda* was actually printing millions of Bibles for distribution to their own Russian people. My spirit had soared in exultation at this remarkable news. Now what?

> The Kingbird had fallen.
>> What would follow?
>>> Only our Father knew the formidable future.
>>>> He knew all about the kingbird in my hand.
>>>>> He knew all about the Kingbird in the Kremlin.

> In that acute awareness my soul is serene.

▪ ▪ ▪

Seventy-two hours later Gorbachev was released. He returned to initiate titanic new changes in the USSR. All the world gasped in awe and wonder.

First
Hint of
Fall

*I*T HAS BEEN AN UNUSUALLY LONG, hot summer. Day after day the rising temperatures have forced Cheri and me to seek relief from the heat downstairs. The whole world seemed to burn beneath the intensity of the relentless sun. Perhaps it is the increasing "hothouse" effect engulfing the planet, or maybe it is the result of unusual weather patterns that fluctuate feverishly. But whatever the cause, we longed for the coolness of fall.

Then yesterday, for the first time, came that touch of Arctic air that promised respite. I went to take a short tramp beside a remote lake high in the hills. The coolness flowed over me in waves of gentle rejuvenation. I inhaled deeply of the sharp, oxygen-charged air. A tremendous exhilaration swept through me. Suddenly I felt stimulated, energetic, alive, strong and eager. It had been months since such strong stimulus stirred my spirit.

There was also utter stillness, serenity, and solitude where I walked beneath the trees. Not a single human footprint had stirred the dust or marked the trail for months. Only deer tracks and chipmunk footprints crossed the path.

In overwhelming gratitude for such pure, undiluted pleasure I lifted my soul in gratitude to my Father. How few people could relish such inspiration, such renewal of body, of soul, of spirit in such a tranquil spot! In utter sincerity I gave thanks for the acute sense of wonder, awe, and powerful presence of Christ my closest companion.

A magnificent golden eagle hunted the rocky crags across the lake. His dark shadow swept along the cliff face, headed south, for already he too sensed winter in the air. A scraggly band of jet-black crows also straggled down the valley in unusual silence, their damage done for the summer. Left behind were their empty nests.

A ruffed grouse exploded out of the brittle under-brush. The sudden noise lasted only split seconds, then all was still again. A family of mergansers riffled the lake. The young were barely able to fly, but in a few weeks their untried wings would carry them south down a hundred waterways.

The whole world was pensive, still, quiet, waiting for the coming of autumn . . . waiting for the full freshness of fall . . . waiting for the transforming impulse of rain and wind that brings autumn's glory.

As I reflected on this, God's gracious Spirit reminded me afresh that it was exactly the same with my own soul. I too was quiet, expectant, waiting for the gentle impress of His renewal. It simply had to be so. It was all a part of His sublime provision for me. The old clinging contamination of life needed to be purged away, cleansed from my conscience, swept clean by the incoming of His own purifying power.

In earnestness, humility, and deep longing the whole of my being was opened to His enfolding presence. "O God," I breathed softly, sincerely, "exchange Your life for mine." Then, bowed gently in His company, my spirit cried out, "Thank You, Father, for filling me with Your Spirit. What a glorious gift!"

In the solitude and in the stillness of that gentle setting my soul was swept clean, purged of all its perverseness, renewed and refreshed beyond words to relate. There came as ever of old that winsome word from Christ: "Abide in me, and I in you."

Not only had there been the first hint of fall in a physical dimension but also that first hint of glory in a divine dimension. I came down off that woodland trail a man renewed without and renewed within.

The Broken Garage Door Opener

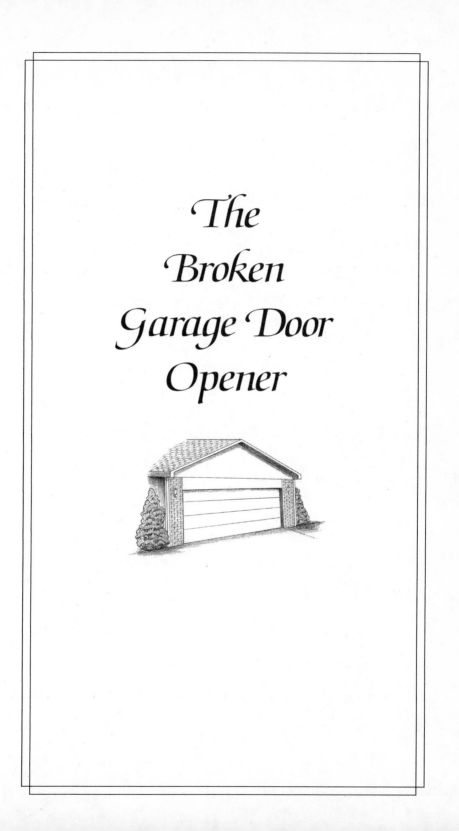

*O*UR EXPERIENCES WITH ELECTRICAL GARAGE DOOR openers have been rather remarkable. The tradesman who installed the first one assured us he had 24 years of experience and we could be sure of trouble-free service. Less than six weeks later I pushed the button to open the door and was greeted with a terrifying crash and splintering of wood.

The unit had torn the great metal door off its brackets bolted to the walls and twisted it so badly that it was impossible to open. The car was imprisoned inside. Only the skilled expertise of a dear friend with the aid of powerful jacks was able to repair the damage and restore the door.

The second home we owned with an electrical garage door opener was in the far north. As long as the weather was warm there were no problems. But with the onset of winter that unit failed to function properly just when one needed it the most. No end of "experts" failed to find the fault. Finally at great cost it was put right by replacing the main circuits.

Two days ago Cheri and I drove into the garage to be greeted by a high-pitched ominous hum. Nothing we did would move that door. This was now the third home in which we faced an electrical problem that was utterly beyond my ability to correct.

We searched through the yellow pages of the phone book. Only one repair man answered, and his shop was over 40 miles away. Calmly he informed me that his charge was 36 dollars an hour from the time he left his premises until he returned. So our bill would be well over 100 dollars just for him to establish the trouble.

I called a kind neighbor who had helped us out before, but he could not come until the next day.

I turned to Ursula and suggested that we quietly entreat our Father for wisdom to repair the unit ourselves. I have no skills or knowledge when it comes to electrical devices, but with divine guidance it was surprising what could be accomplished.

We stood quietly in the garage and asked our Father in audible terms to direct me in what to do. I climbed a stepladder, carefully cleaned off the mechanism, and examined its drive chain. It seemed under tremendous stress. So I decided to move it ahead another notch on the drive sprocket. At once the door responded to the touch of the button. But it would not close properly. Cheri read some further instructions in the operator's manual. By trial and error we twisted and twirled various knobs and buttons.

Suddenly the door shut precisely as it should and opened exactly as it was designed to do. We were ecstatic!

Just at that very moment our neighbor drove into the driveway. He was just as delighted as we were. All three of us embraced each other and gave hearty thanks for the guidance that God our Father had supplied. How grateful and glad we were to be led so surely in such a tricky and difficult repair.

Yes, He is here, He is dear; no need to fear.
Yet so often we forget.
How human we are!

Peace

*J*UST A FEW MOMENTS AGO I went to stand at the window overlooking our "wild garden" of sagebrush, greasewood, and bunch grass. As I stood there drenching my soul in the cool freshness of dawn a fairly large bird fluttered down out of the morning sky. It alighted right in front of me. It was a magnificent mourning dove . . . one of the most beloved of our desert birds. Quietly it set about searching for grass seeds on the ground.

What a beautiful omen with which to begin a new day at the very outset of a new week! In stillness of spirit there swept through my person a surge of quiet gratitude: "Thank You, Father, for Your feathered minstrel of peace."

It reminded me afresh of a moving occasion about two years ago when the young pastor of a church we attended in California felt distraught in spirit. His work was not going well. It seemed he would be driven from his church. Everything seemed so dark! He went out to walk alone in the grounds of the sanctuary, and to pray. As he did so, suddenly a beautiful wild dove fluttered down out of the trees and alighted on his shoulder. The bird appeared perfectly at peace. And suddenly, so was he. "I am with you always" were the words which swept into his soul. In that brief encounter with the wild bird his faith was rekindled.

Openly, honestly, without shame he stood before his people the next day and told them about the dove. He is still serving the same church to this day and it flourishes under God's gracious care.

The other evening, after an unusually warm day, Ursula threw open our great front door at dusk. The cool air flowing down the high ridges behind us drifted into the house and refreshed the atmosphere.

Suddenly there was a smooth, swift, swish of a dark blue-and-brown bird that swept into the living room. A lovely, graceful barn swallow circled over our heads briefly, then flew back out over the lawns. Momentarily both of us were breathless with surprise and delight. What a beautiful messenger bearing good cheer. "Yes—I am here—all is well!" We needed no more.

Just yesterday I commenced a series of special Bible studies in a community down the valley. They are open to any and all who may care to come. I am especially keen to reach the unchurched, who have never known the gentle touch of The Master's hand upon their hearts and lives. His messengers of peace assure me He is among us to speak peace to any who hear Him say, "BE NOT AFRAID!"

A
Sudden
Surprise

$\mathcal{F}$OR 40 LONG AND SOMETIMES PAINFUL years, Ursula had been cut off from the land of her childhood in Eastern Germany. First the formidable Iron Curtain of Communist control made any return impossible. Then the erection of the brutal Berlin Wall of concrete, steel, and barbed wire barred her reentry. And even after that came crashing down, there were complications of one sort and another that prevented her free passage to the place of her birth.

Just 18 months ago all her diligent efforts to obtain a proper visa for reentry were dashed to pieces. She endured the disappointment with a sweet spirit of resignation, so I assured her that somehow soon, in an unexpected and lovely surprise, our Father would open the way for her. And He did, in His own gentle manner.

Just a few days ago a young neighbor lady, who comes from a German family, stopped at our door and simply asked Ursula to accompany her back to Germany. It was all so sudden, so surprising, so exciting. She was sure they could secure special, reduced-price air tickets the very next morning. And they did, for roughly half the cost of a regular fare. Added to this, Ursula was able to pick up a Eurorail pass for a very special price, which included a free boat excursion down the Rhine River. In a matter of hours all the necessary travel arrangements were completed at roughly 50 percent of the usual cost, all at the choicest fall season of the year.

Five days later the two ladies flew off, free as birds, happy and excited as a couple of schoolgirls. Best of all, this time there were absolutely no travel restrictions, no police surveillance, and no official reports to make. How dear and gracious and all-knowing is our Father!

All of this was a special bonus from our Father for the simple reason that first we had to build a bridge of love to this young woman who invited Ursula to go with her. When first we came to live here she was rather shy and quiet. Quite obviously she did not wish to associate with us, feeling that somehow we might look with contempt upon her.

But we persisted in reaching out to her and to her family with goodwill and good cheer. No stone was left unturned in our endeavors to show an interest in their lives and to bring help, joy, and love into their affairs. Bit by bit the barriers, as formidable at first as the Berlin Wall itself, were broken down with kindness. Little by little, compassion, concern, and good cheer dispelled her distrust. By and by the love of Christ swept away her apprehension and she began to warm to us.

Eventually we found out that her aged grandma in Germany was a dear, devout woman who truly loved the Lord. In fact when she came to Canada for a wee visit we were warmly drawn to each other. Then one lovely day the dear soul suddenly realized that one of the books they had been studying in her Bible class at home was a German translation of one of my works. She was beside herself with delight.

So it is that in His own wondrous ways our Father works behind the scenes to draw us to Himself. As someone said to me just a short time ago, He never slumbers, He never goes on strike, and He never takes time out for coffee. He is always active on our behalf!

Little wonder that life with Him is so replete with sudden surprises, joyous interludes, and deep delight. What an adventure to have Him share our days and fill our hours with beautiful bonuses of His design!

In wonder, awe, and humble gratitude we bow our spirits and give Him honor with thanksgiving.

■ ■ ■

Some two weeks later the small plane carrying Ursula home swept swiftly and smoothly out of the evening sky to land safely on the runway outside our tiny air terminal. She was the first one off. Her radiant smile and jaunty steps assured me all was well. In a matter of moments we were caught up in each other's arms. It was the culmination of a lovely chapter in her life.

Along the way our Lord had brought kind strangers across her path to help her in her travels. There had been a remarkable and jubilant reunion with her childhood chum. The two girls had grown up together in the Christian orphanage, becoming dearer to each other than even filial sisters. Now, after a separation of more than 40 years, they were back together again, laughing, chatting, reminiscing in that joyous way which touches the deepest wellsprings of human affection. Some nights they lay awake until three in the morning reliving the distant days of girlhood. They prayed together, sang together, walked together—lost in the love and loyalty that some 40 years of Communism could not quench.

As a beautiful bonus, Ursula was also able to visit special places of interest she had often dreamed of seeing in her own native land. There was a tranquil interlude on the borders of Austria and Switzerland with the Alps in the distance; a serene, gentle excursion up the Rhine River with its castles, vineyards, and picturesque country villages; even a special feast of wild mushrooms which she used to collect as a child in the woods . . . a rare and special delicacy.

Perhaps most astonishing, she came home with half her spending money still safe in her bulging purse!

Such are the sudden surprises and profound pleasures which our Father is pleased to bestow on those who wait upon Him.

Wood Harvest

*I*N OUR PART OF THE WESTERN mountains, local residents are allowed to go into the forests to collect their own winter wood. Only two simple rules apply: Any trees cut up for firewood must be either dead or already fallen on the forest floor. So the search for suitable trees is a bit of an adventure that always sharpens the fall season.

Yesterday was a day that a friend and I had set aside for woodcutting. We left soon after daybreak. There was a sharp nip in the air, ideal for heavy work. The truck growled its way up the twisting mountain road until we were far above the valley. Larches, poplars, and sumac flamed with fire in their October colors. They had been touched with frost and set alight with autumn sunshine.

Sure enough, we soon stumbled across a stately stand of tall pines, some of which had been killed by the deadly bark beetles. To our delight they were within easy reach of the road. In minutes the chain saw roared into pulsing power. Its superbly sharpened cutting teeth sliced through the wood almost like a knife cutting cheese. By noon, our backs aching and our hands and arms crying for relief, we had the truck loaded to capacity. What a windfall for a couple of old codgers well into their seventies!

Just as we were dusting off our trousers from sawdust, dirt, and chips of bark a gnarled old cattle rancher drove up. "What you two young bucks up to?" He grinned mischievously and I laughed at him in glee. "Just proving we can still hold our own with the best of them up in these hills!" He roared his approval. "It looks to me like you could lick most of these lazy young fellows that just hang around town looking for a handout!"

With that he put his rough rig in gear and roared off up the hills to hunt for his stubborn steers.

Gently we nursed the huge load of wood down the rutted road for home. It would keep winter at bay, and warm our home through a hundred stormy nights.

Ursula served us a delicious meal of soup, sliced turkey, cheese, cranberry sauce, and home-baked scones. I was almost too weary to eat, but my spirit soared with gratitude for such a generous supply of wood.

After lunch the three of us unloaded the tired truck. Carefully we stacked the fragrant fuel along the rough walls of the garage. There its rich aroma would pervade the place; there it would remain crisp and dry all season; and there it would be split to give me sturdy winter exercise.

The wood harvest was complete. Just the sight of the creamy white wood stacked high at home was enough to provide a profound feeling of deep well-being. Toil and sweat and straining muscles had all turned into serene satisfaction.

All of them were good gifts, gentle gifts, yes, generous gifts from our Father. He had grown the trees untended by any man. He had sent rain, snow, mist, and sunshine to nourish the forest. He had painted the hills in their autumn glory. He had led us to this stand of tall pines. He had given us the strength and skill to harvest the wood. Now He would give us the deep delight of relishing its warmth. His bounties come new each day.

Last night, in perfect peace, I slept like a log!
This morning every ache is gone.
My strength is renewed as a youth.
All are good gifts from Him.

The
Power of
Encouragement

*I*T SEEMS TO ME THAT PERHAPS the most precious gift that one person can bestow upon another is gentle encouragement. The humble yet noble art of helping another human being over the hard place and out of the deep ditch is one of the rare attributes which can inject both joy and satisfaction into our few years here.

It is with the deepest gratitude of fondest affection that I recall those men and women who in my dark days drew near to encourage me. Who were not afraid to fortify my faith in God, my Father. Who were loving enough to come over and laugh with me and so help lift the load a bit. Who cared to the point where they would put pen to paper in order to tell me I in turn had cheered them in their distress or strengthened them in their resolve to push ahead.

Yesterday such a letter came from a minister whom I have never even met. He is the chairman of a committee which has invited me to go down to the lower mainland and address over 100 pastors who are getting together for mutual encouragement in God's service. They are of all denominations.

His closing remark expresses the reason they asked me to come: "Thank you for being willing to come and address a group of men and women who need people such as yourself to keep them encouraged in their ministries." What a noble call! What a profound responsibility! What a charge to carry out before my Master and those in His service!

My first reaction to this call was to decline the duty, and withdraw in apprehension from its stern demands. But God's gracious Spirit constrained me to be strong and of good courage in Christ. I was not to be afraid nor dismayed, even though I was an ordinary layperson speaking to well over 100 full-time professional preachers. Such were the mysteries of the Most High. He would not leave me nor forsake me. I was His messenger.

I went to walk alone in the hills. There had to be a rock-solid assurance from my Father that He knew the deepest needs of these pastors. He alone knew the exact message best suited to encourage them in their work in our weary old world. He knew how it should be delivered and the unshakable truth upon which it should stand.

Within an hour I came down off the slopes quietly convinced of the precise theme for the convocation: "CALM CONFIDENCE IN CHRIST FOR THE DAY." What could be more encouraging? What could be said that would put more steel in a person's spine, more flame in his faith, more energy in his enthusiasm to exalt and uplift Christ Himself?

In this humble, simple, forthright way He in turn would draw perishing people to Himself. His ministers would be encouraged. His grand, good work would be done in their day.

From within my soul there welled up that superb, acute awareness: "O Christ, You are here; all is well." There is nothing so reassuring in all the world! There permeated my spirit the profound peace which only He can bestow on us common people. And accompanying both of these was that sure strength of His abundant life pervading all of my life. Christ in you!

In serenity and stillness I sat down at my desk and wrote a very brief note of acceptance. The Most High had called me to encourage His ministers. I was at His command. The charge would be taken up. Like the craggy old Caleb in Joshua's day I would cry out to my contemporaries, "Give me this mountain!"

The mountain of despair to dispel.
The mountain of discouragement to dismiss.
The mountain of darkness to destroy.

Is anything too hard for the Lord? No, no, no! One common man in company with Christ is a majority.

Fallen Leaves, Fallen Trees

*E*VERY AUTUMN, ON A STILL, GOLDEN day, without wind, I make a private pilgrimage to a rushing mountain river that tumbles out of the mountains west of us. I go alone for several reasons. First to find serene solitude in a superb setting of wild and unspoiled wilderness. Secondly to celebrate the pure ecstasy of fall in all the splendor of its flaming foliage and gorgeous carpet of pastel colors on the forest floor. Thirdly in fond memory of one of my dearest friends who loved this range so fervently. We often came here together. His ashes are scattered on the meadows above tree line. Lastly I come for a few fleeting hours to be utterly still in spirit so that my Father can converse with me quietly.

Yesterday was that day!

It startled me to find the first snow of the season already settled like a thin veil of white over the ridges. Only three days ago it had been so hot that ranchers and orchardists in the valley had their irrigation sprinklers going with full force. But yesterday the skies were heavy with dark clouds. Mixed rain and sleet drifted down softly from the overcast. Not a soul stirred in the stillness. All morning not another person moved in my mountain realm. It was almost as if it was the beginning of time, before people crowded the planet.

I pulled on my old, comfortable, sun-bleached Stetson. Its faded wool fabric, stained with a hundred hard climbs, felt so comfortable. For the first time this fall it was a pleasure to fit my rough hands into warm, lined gloves. Rough bush pants covered my wool long johns. Double wool sweaters enfolded my chest beneath a tough old windbreaker that had carried me snugly through a score of storms.

With binoculars in hand and a spring in my step I set off softly along the edge of the mountain torrent. I was deep in thought.

A flood of vivid memories came back to me. There was the first trek I ever made into these wild ranges on horseback. The time when I was so moved by the majesty and might of the Cathedral Range that I began a crusade to have the area set aside as a Provincial Park. This eventually became a living, winsome reality. I recalled the day I came across 16 bighorn rams grazing near the summit in a storm. Suddenly the clouds parted and a brilliant rainbow arched over the scene in breathtaking beauty. I relived the last time my friend and I climbed here in deep snow on a brilliant blue day, watching a band of mule deer and listening to the coyotes call.

Yes, magnificent, moving memories unfolded before me. They were a vivid, rich reminder of just how thrilling my life had been. So full of adventure, of joy, of excitement, yes, of wondrous contentment. Surely my days had been as bountiful as a great balm of Gilead in luxuriant growth beside these rushing mountain waters. But now I was in the autumn of my years. To everything there is a season. And the searching thought came to my questing soul: "How soon now will it be before the last vestige of your vitality flutters down to earth like a golden leaf from one of these giant poplars?"

With head bowed I strolled softly through the drifts of bronze and golden leaves. They were piled against fallen tree trunks, wedged among the rocks, spread out in golden carpets on the mountain track. I picked up several and admired their color. It would be their last burst of beauty. In a few days they would begin to decay where they lay. Dew and dampness, earthworms, forest fungus, soil bacteria, and micro-organisms would begin to break them down into fertile humus that would nourish a new forest.

This was true of more than just fallen leaves; it was equally so of fallen trees, broken branches, and other windblown debris that littered the forest floor. Here lay the raw material of birth, life, death, and rebirth from which would spring new plants, sturdy shrubs, young seedlings, and a whole new forest in the years ahead—all because these trees had lived and died in their own brief glory, and were carried away at last when their work was done, in the powerful sweep of wind from the high slopes above.

The clear, pungent, profound thought swept through my own spirit—not with any sense of melancholy or remorse, but rather with glad rejoicing: "You have lived a full and robust life. Your years have been replete with high adventure and joyous good cheer. You have been acutely conscious of the presence and power of The Most High, who has enriched your sojourn here. Now the time draws near for your story to end. But out of its experiences new life of eternal worth will come to others who follow in your footsteps."

Like fallen leaves and fallen trees it is not in vain:
For this is the basis upon which others grow.
Yellow leaves and brown forest duff give new
life.
And out of our past others will prosper.
It is ever, always, that way with our
Father.
No leaf falls to the earth unnoticed.
Each is a part of His grand design.

I walked on softly, my leather footwear scuffling through the autumn gold. A few stray leaves of red osier dogwood fluttered in the gentle breeze along the river's edge. It was like a quiet salute to a soul deep in communion with Christ. "Heaven and earth shall pass away . . . but I remain eternal, unchanging . . . the enduring entity in the cosmos . . . and because I live, you too shall live forever."

Therein lay the supreme secret to all of life: I IN HIM, HE IN ME.

With sweet assurance and superb serenity of spirit I came down out of the hills. All was well. He is here!

World
Series
Climax

$\mathcal{F}$OR THE BETTER PART OF A week we had watched the titanic struggle for supremacy in the World Series. The Atlanta Braves and the Minnesota Twins were both Cinderella teams. Each had come from last to first in their respective leagues. Both had shown amazing tenacity in hanging on when it seemed all hope of winning was gone. Now they were locked in a final contest to decide the issue of which team would take home the World Series trophy.

Uncounted millions of viewers from all over the world watched and waited with bated breath. Fans cheered and fans cried. Coaches and managers and players chewed their gum, chewed their tobacco, and chewed their finger-nails. Bats were broken; bases were stolen; home runs soared over the walls; foul hits flew into the grandstands; incredible pitches were thrown and unbelievable catches were made all over the fields. But still the series was locked in suspense. There had never been such a baseball spectacle in all the glorious history of the game. Night after night every person in the stadium had stayed shouting and screaming until after midnight.

Then came Saturday evening. It was the sixth game in the best of seven series. The Braves led by three games to two. It was imperative that the Twins pull this one out of the fire to tie the match at three games each. But it seemed the fierce duel would go on all night. Nine innings, ten innings, eleven innings—nothing decided, every player taut as a superstar. Then came the bottom of the twelfth. Kirby Puckett, powerful as a massive Brahman bull, stepped up to the plate. The ball hurtled toward him. With one mighty stroke and crack of the bat he rocketed the ball over the wall.

In a single shot the score was evened. The crowd went wild. And at three games each the players leaped with ecstasy into each other's arms. Sunday's seventh game would decide the winner.

But Sunday was also to be the final evening of our fall series of Bible classes. I wondered to myself if anyone would be interested enough to tear himself away from the television screen to turn up for a two-hour Bible study at the same identical time. Where were people's priorities? It would be a marvel if anyone cared enough, on this memorable night, to even drive through the dark and show up at the church.

But they did—all sorts of people. A surprising number of sturdy souls cared more about eternal truth than the passions of the playing field. It was astonishing to see so many men there. Old men, younger men. Men who would normally be glued to the tube. Surely, yes, surely Christ had moved among us as of old, and folks had found in Him nourishment for their spirits that was equal to or better than any stimulation that baseball could offer.

The class carried on for its full time. The studies were not cut short to accommodate the game. It was clear that we were putting first things first. At last the session ended. We parted with fond farewells, climbed into our ice-cold cars, and headed home through the deep darkness of the northern night.

Entering the house, warm and inviting, I felt sure the final game was long since over. But when we flicked on the TV switch, we found that the score was still 0–0 at the end of the ninth inning. It was almost beyond belief! What a matchup—three games each and again 0–0!

Quickly, in her happy brisk way, Ursula boiled water for a hot cup of tea and laid out home-baked bread with hot sausages, and we settled down in happy contentment to watch the game. In His generous generosity our Father had given us this joyous surprise.

Again the final game was settled with a single swing of the bat, a mighty dash for home plate by Tom Gladden, and a leading score of 1–0 for the home team, the Twins.

Kelly, their manager, remarked afterward, "This was a World Series in which, really, both teams had won!" Both clubs had refused to give ground, and both leagues could look with honor on the performance of their players. Both were covered with glory.

Deep down inside I felt exactly the same about loyal people who had come to the Bible classes. They were just as enthusiastic baseball fans as those who had stayed home. But they were equally eager Bible fans who would put their priorities in proper order and play the game of life to the hilt.

In His gracious generosity God Himself had truly honored them as they had honored Him. For they had come up winners, having enjoyed the best of both activities. That night my spirit soared in upwelling gratitude and humble thanks for sturdy people who could be brave enough to put Christ first. Yet they still shared in the pure pleasure of being a part of the exciting climax of the greatest World Series ever staged.

In His gentle, tender, understanding ways our Father has His stirring strategy of filling our cups to overflowing. He arranges for us to drink deeply from the pure waters of His own refreshing presence. But likewise He allows us to drink deeply from the sweet streams of noble human endeavor.

Because of both, our strength is renewed, our hopes soar high, and we are refreshed.

Flight to the Eagle's Nest

$\mathcal{W}$E CALL IT "THE EAGLE'S NEST" simply because, for Ursula and me, it is a quiet sanctuary set apart high in the heart of the Canadian Rockies. Also because the windows look out over a giant grove of gnarled poplars where bald eagles rest in surprising numbers.

For months we had looked forward to a quiet week in this gentle spot with the snow-draped ranges all around us. But in the meantime there were other, more important matters to claim our time: commitments to teach Bible classes all through the fall season; another manuscript to complete, correspondence to answer; and all the usual seasonal chores around a northern home.

As the season progressed, the weather suddenly began to deteriorate alarmingly. A very sudden, sharp drop in temperatures quick-froze all the lush green foliage on the trees and shrubs. It was as if there had been no preparation for the early arrival of the Arctic air mass. Almost overnight the whole region was in the grip of ice and frost.

With this sudden plunge into winter weather came the inevitable snow sweeping in over the mountains from the dark, grey expanse of the Gulf of Alaska. The high country was blanketed with deep drifts driven by the wind. Mountain roads began to be hazardous, and we wondered what driving would be like when the time came for our "flight to The Eagle's Nest."

Quietly, like two small trusting children, we turned the whole matter over to our Father. He knew full well how much we needed this little respite. He could prepare the way for us. He could lead us there in peace. And He did!

As dawn broke on the day we were to leave, I stepped outside to check the weather. From a lifetime in the high country I could sense at once it would be a glorious day.

The overcast was lifting. The wind had shifted to the southwest. Stars were beginning to shine through the opening rifts in the clouds. This would be a magnificent day with silver linings.

Just at daybreak we were packed and on our way. The Sonata soared up the almost-empty highway headed north and east. The roads were bare, swept clean by the fierce wind. And wonder of wonders, the sun broke over the eastern ranges to flood our whole realm in lovely golden light.

In her usual jaunty way, eyes sparkling, Ursula quoted one of her favorite old-time folk sayings: "When angels travel, the sky always smiles!" It made me smile as well and we chuckled together with good cheer.

After two hours of steady driving we stopped on the shores of a deep lake for a hot drink. Our fresh brew out of our thermos was delectable. We stretched our legs with a brisk walk while munching a tasty sandwich that Ursula had tucked in our picnic basket.

Our spirits soared in gratitude. What a glorious day! It really was a minor miracle for a couple of God's

own children. In unison, spontaneously, we began to sing
that dear old song, "Oh what a beautiful morning, Oh
what a beautiful day!"

Steadily, surely, the highway climbed into higher
and higher terrain. And still the surface was free of snow
and the whole winter world was bright with sunlight. It
was like driving in a dream: blue skies, sparkling streams
decorated with fringes of ice, soaring peaks shining white
under new snow, trees and shrubs silver-coated with fresh
frost—an ever-changing panorama of pure splendor and
inspiring glory.

To our surprise we had seen wild mountain bighorns
on the open slopes. Noisy flocks of wild Canada geese
were flying down the valleys, and blue jays were everywhere. A pleasant little encounter was with a handsome
coyote hunting mice at the edge of the road. I had spotted
him far ahead, so I slowed down as we drew near him
with quiet respect. He was dressed in magnificent fur of
unusual warm, fawn colors. He bounded into the shelter
of a thick alder thicket and looked at us with wonder in
his deep brown eyes. He was a splendid specimen of his
own sturdy species.

Never had I seen these mountain ranges in pure,
clear light of such intensity. So often mist, sleet, cloud
cover, and blowing snow obscured the peaks. We stopped
again and again to take in breathtaking vistas. The photographs would be lifelong mementos of this incredible
journey to our "Eagle's Nest."

We traversed the highest passes with remarkable
ease. Deep snow clung to the trees and rocks and dwarf
shrubs on the lofty alpine slopes. But still the road was
bare, dry, and safe as any summer drive. What joy, what
rest, what pure pleasure! In stunning, vivid, clear recol-
lection my memory recalled the first major photographic
expedition I had made into this region 35 years ago.

There had been no highway over the mountains
then. I hiked in all alone, a huge backpack weighing
me down. I was in search of grizzly bears, and I found

them in this formidable wilderness. Again I relived the
afternoon I spent following a huge male, a bright golden
patch on his great chest, who thrilled me with his
awesome grandeur. The final picture of him was taken
at less than 20 feet. Then we parted in peace amid a world
of glaciers, snowfields, and rushing ice-fed streams.

Yes, the mountain realm had changed a lot since
then. But in His generous kindness, my Father had
arranged for still another day of splendor to stir my soul
again as of old.

Hour after hour we soared across the slopes, down
the valleys, and into the remote region where our "Eagle's
Nest" awaited us. The last long shafts of golden sunset lit
up the western peaks of the Rockies as we pulled into our
place of rest.

True to form, a magnificent bald eagle was perched
in the bare-limbed poplars. Others circled over the river
ponds and shallows, plucking the deep-red spawning
kokanee from the icy water. Ravens and crows, coyotes
and mink were all finding a fall feast along the stream
banks. As Ursula put it so succinctly, "This is easy
fishing!"

We settled cozily into our snug, warm nest with a
hot bowl of soup, home-baked bread, and steaming cups
of tea. We sensed a sweet serenity of spirit within. Oh
how gentle, how gracious, how joyous were the quiet
adventures of life in company with Christ! In genuine
gratitude we embraced each other in warm hugs, giving
hearty thanks for an unforgettable day.

For us this was a joyous thanksgiving, shaped by
the natural wonders and pure pleasure of our Father's
arrangement. We were rich beyond belief in fond memories and deep delight which only He could provide.

Contentment

*C*ONTENTMENT IS REALLY A MULTICOLORED QUILT woven
from the varied strands of life's daily experiences. It
is the fabric fashioned from the simple joys of our days,
the gentle love of other human beings and the quiet
repose we find in Christ our dearest Friend.

This book is a humble collection of little vignettes
which have been written to describe the quiet contentment
of our life. There is nothing spectacular nor sensational
about these events. They are homespun strands woven
into our lives during the past year. Our Father has been
the Master Weaver. It has been wonderful to watch Him at
work. Even out of the drab days He has drawn a silver
edge that has stilled our souls in gratitude.

Contentment comes in a hundred hues. Here are
but a few.

> The snug warmth of a well-built home keeping
>   winter weather at bay.
>
> The fragrance of fir and pine burning brightly.

The fit of a familiar, well-worn jacket that has withstood a hundred storms.

Cups of hot tea and bowls of steaming soup shared with friends around the kitchen nook.

The calm, sure awareness of Christ's presence in the room, in the garden, on the road, or in the hills.

The stillness of a star-studded night in black velvet.

The sweet melodies of fine music stirring my soul. Old refrains full of refreshing messages from The Most High.

Hearty laughter and high humor with deep chuckles.

The warm grip of a friend's hand, the fond embrace that speaks solace to the soul.

The serene assurance that comes from ruminating in God's Word. The sure guidance of His gracious Spirit.

The surge of new strength and fresh vigor that put a spring in our step, a sparkle in our eyes, a smile on our lips.

The exquisite taste of clean, cool water, of fresh fruit, of newly harvested vegetables.

The happy, unexpected surprises that come in the mail by letter or across the miles by phone reminding us that others care, and pray, and share their love.

The serene sense of repose that comes from being right with God my Father, right with others, right with my self . . . and creative in His care.

The joyous daily delight of knowing that Christ Himself is here, and all is well!